# Decentralized Finance (DeFi) 2023

# A Beginners Guide On Investing, Blockchain, Smart Contracts, Peer To Peer, Borrow, Save, Trade, Cryptocurrency, Bitcoin, Ethereum, Altcoin & Yield Farming

# Table of Contents

# Introduction

Decentralized finance refers the ecosystem of decentralized financial applications (dapps) on the blockchain.

In this ecosystem of services without an intermediary, it is possible for anyone to interact with the different protocols to ask for loans, exchange tokens or assets, create tokens that represent real estate or real assets to sell them, rent their assets in exchange for interest .... and much more.

It is a constantly evolving world that in a few years is progressing in an impressive way involving more and more projects, people and money. To operate in this decentralized set of services there is no need for authorization from a central body such as a bank.

It is transparent, verifiable and available to everyone. Today, there are many barriers that prevent all people from enjoying certain financial services. Suffice it to say that a third world citizen does not have the ability to open bank accounts easily, or ask for a loan or invest in assets.

With DeFi, no one cares who you are or where you live, the doors are open to everyone with low costs and very high security. Anyone with an internet connection can access financial services such as Dex, stablecoins, synthetic assets (stocks, indices ...), insurance ...Users maintain full control over their resources and interact autonomously with the different protocols.

In traditional finance, you must trust an institution; in decentralized finance, math has to be trusted. It is all governed by code and mathematics (code is law), upon the occurrence of such an event there is the consequence X.

No surprises or unexpected in DeFi, no account blocked for verification or investigation by a central authority. There are only the people and the protocol.

An example to understand on the fly are the DEX (decentralized exchanges).

If we want to exchange a token for another, it will be enough for us to interact with the DEX, provide our token to the Smart contract and take the corresponding token we want from the smart contract that was previously provided by another person.

# 1. Understanding Decentralized Finance (Defi)

Decentralized finance (Defi) is a popular blockchain-based financial infrastructure. In general, the word refers to a protocol stack that is open, permissionless, and highly interoperable and is based on public smart contract platforms such as the Ethereum blockchain. It's a more open and transparent version of present financial services. Defi isn't dependent on middlemen or centralized organizations in particular. Instead, open protocols and decentralized apps are used (DApps). Code enforces agreements, safe and verifiable transactions are performed, and approved state changes are recorded on a public blockchain.

As a result, this architecture has the ability to generate an unalterable and highly interoperable financial system with unparalleled clarity, equal access rights, and minimal need for custodians, central clearinghouses, or escrow services, as "smart contracts" can handle the majority of these functions. For example, one can buy USD-pegged assets (so-called stablecoins) on decentralized exchanges.

All Defi protocols and applications are built on smart contracts. Smart contracts are small applications that are stored on a blockchain and run concurrently by a large number of validators. The network is built in the context of public blockchains so that each participant can participate in and verify the accurate execution of each action. As a consequence, as compared to conventional centralized computing, smart contracts are relatively inefficient. Smart contracts provide a high degree of security since they always function as stated, enabling anybody to independently verify the state changes that result. When executed properly, smart contracts are highly transparent and limit the possibility of manipulation and arbitrary interference.

To understand the uniqueness of smart contracts, we must first investigate standard server-based web apps. When a person interacts with such an app, they cannot see the program's underlying logic. In addition, the user has no influence over the execution environment. Either (or both) of these could be tampered with. As a result, the user must have faith in the application service provider. Both difficulties are addressed by smart contracts, which ensure that an application runs as planned. The contract code is kept on the underlying blockchain, making it publicly accessible. The contract's behavior is deterministic, and thousands of network members process function calls (in the form of transactions) in parallel, assuring the execution's legality. When the execution causes state changes, such as account balance changes, the blockchain network's consensus rules apply, and the changes are recorded in and protected by the blockchain's state tree.

Because smart contracts have access to a wide instruction set, they are highly customizable. They may also act as a custodian for crypto assets, with completely customizable criteria for how, when, and to whom they are transferred.

This paves the way for a slew of new applications and ecosystems to emerge. For the first time, Szabo coined the term "smart contract." Szabo went on to say that many agreements might be "hidden in the hardware and software we interact with, in such a manner as to make a breach of contract expensive...for the breacher," citing a vending machine as an example. Buterin proposed a decentralized blockchain-based smart contract platform to address trust issues regarding the execution environment and enable secure execution (composability). Wood formalized the concept and implemented it under the name Ethereum. Ethereum is the most prominent smart contract platform in terms of market value, viable applications, and development activity despite various competitors.

Defi is still a niche industry with modest volumes, but this is changing rapidly. The total amount of money invested in Defi-related smart contracts has topped $10 billion. It is crucial to realize that these are not metrics for transaction volume or market capitalization; the term "value" refers to reserves held in smart contracts that may be used in various ways as described throughout this book.

## How Does Defi Work?

From a technical perspective, Defi is a group of decentralized applications (dApps) primarily running on the Ethereum smart contract ecosystem that provides blockchain-based financial services without intermediaries. Therefore, understanding how Defi works requires knowledge pertaining to three important topics: blockchain technology, Ethereum, and smart contracts.

Blockchain

Blockchain technology is the foundation for not only Defi but everything related to cryptocurrencies as well. In short, blockchains are digital ledgers that permanently record immutable data made out of publicly shared blocks with everyone.

Bitcoin, the first blockchain network, was launched in 2009 and is a game-changing idea because of security and scarcity.

Security

Blockchain networks like Bitcoin utilize the Proof of Work (PoW) consensus mechanism to execute transactions. PoW entails the employment of energy and hardware power by users known as miners to solve difficult mathematical problems in exchange for incentives earned by confirming blocks.

A block is a collection of signed transactions submitted by ordinary users who wish to send their money. Each transaction has a hash that verifies its ledger chronological sequence. As a result, each block has its hash linked to the preceding block's hash, creating a sequential chain of blocks.

It is almost difficult to attack Bitcoin since the whole ledger (a blockchain's transaction history) is spread in the form of copies across thousands of nodes. To create a new consensus and agree to a different version of the blockchain, a malevolent person would need to control more than 50% of the network's nodes (devices operated by miners).

Scarcity

Bitcoin is limited because there is a finite number of coins available. Unlike fiat currencies, it is impossible to manufacture and issue new coins indefinitely on the blockchain since the restriction is built into the cryptocurrency. Only 21 million Bitcoin will ever exist, and as more miners put coins onto the market, the circulating supply will steadily grow.

Scarcity enables Bitcoin to function as a store-of-value asset, which means it can be used as a haven or hedge in times of need, which is why investors refer to Bitcoin as "digital gold." When combined with excellent cryptographic security, scarcity makes Bitcoin one of the best-performing investment assets of all time.

**Ethereum** & Smart Contracts

Ethereum and Smart Contracts Ethereum is another cryptocurrency that adds to the usefulness of blockchain technology by using smart contracts, which are written in the Solidity programming language and used to build a rich dApp ecosystem with on-chain functionality other than payments.

Smart contracts, as previously said, are self-executing computer programs that operate autonomously and activate based on preset circumstances. Smart contracts provide significant advantages such as decentralization, security, and transparency, despite their slower execution speed when compared to centralized data systems.

Anyone can see and analyze the code of a smart contract to see whether it is malicious or not, which is a stark contrast to the banking industry. Furthermore, smart contracts do not take sides and only perform what they are instructed, ensuring that an Ethereum transaction will never take an unexpected turn.

Smart contracts are third-party mediators that handle transactions and agreements reached by at least two people. They eliminate the requirement for trust in an otherwise trustless system by allowing users to employ smart contracts instead of depending on the other party's good faith. They also let users avoid centralized middlemen like exchanges and banks, which would normally assist them with on-chain transactions.

To conclude, Ethereum may be seen as a smart contract-enabled version of Bitcoin, allowing it to execute computational logic and enable functionalities otherwise unavailable in first-generation blockchains.

Gas Fees

Users engage directly with smart contracts in Defi; thus, there are no gas fees. All of the goods and services are non-custodial, which means that assets may stay in the user's wallet rather than being deposited on the platform. A person may, for example, exchange tokens on Uniswap straight from his MetaMask.wallet. The disputed coins are never stored in Uniswap's native crypto wallets. The tokens are instead exchanged for other tokens in the exchange's smart contracts.

While the noncustodial feature increases the degree of decentralization in Defi, it comes at a high cost, which may discourage investors. A centralized exchange typically processes internal transactions to transfer assets, with no extra costs other than the trading fees. Because a DEX does not store the assets directly and requires the user to engage with smart contracts, all transactions are subject to Ethereum's gas fees.

## How Ethereum Gas Power Transactions

All blockchain networks are supported by miners, a group of users who host nodes and confirm transactions. Blockchains must compensate miners with transaction fees to attract them and allow them to function in the first place.

On Ethereum, transaction costs are referred to as gas fees. Every conceivable smart contract transaction or activity, like as moving tokens, verifying balances, executing a smart contract function, and so on, consumes gas.

Another function of gas is that it establishes priority for various tasks. The greater the expense, the more difficult the job. As a result, gas acts as a limit, preventing the network from being overburdened by low-cost, basic operations.

When there aren't enough miners, and Ethereum sees a spike in activity, the blockchain encounters a phenomenon known as network congestion. Gas costs soar at that point, and the gas price for all transactions rises as well. Congestion on the network may persist for weeks, if not months, and the blockchain's status can only revert to normal if demand decreases. Fees may run from $40 to $100 per transaction, if not more, in certain instances. Because fees make for a major part of their transactions, investors who trade small sizes are naturally inclined to pause their Defi activity during this time.

## How Decentralized Is Defi?

It's difficult to say how decentralized Defi is. For the purpose of simplicity, we shall divide decentralization into three categories: centralized, semi-decentralized, and entirely decentralized.

1. Centralized
    - Features: Custodial, centralized price feeds, centralized interest rates, and centralized liquidity for margin calls.
    - Examples include Celsius, Nexo, BlockFi, and Salt.
2. Decentralized to a degree (has one or more of these characteristics but not all)
    - Features: Decentralized platform development/updates, decentralized interest rate determination, permissionless margin liquidity, permissionless initiation of margin calls, decentralized price feeds, noncustodial
    - Examples include bZx, dYdX, MakerDAO, Compound.
3. Completely Decentralized
    - Features: All the components are decentralized
    - Examples include: No Defi protocol is completely decentralized yet.

## The Defi Dashboard

A dashboard is a simple platform that centralizes all of your Defi activities. It is a great tool for seeing and tracking the location of your assets across various Defi protocols. The dashboard can categorize your assets into many categories, such as deposits, debt, and investments.

When you access your dashboard, you will typically be required to provide your Ethereum address (e.g.: 0x4Cdc86fa95Ec2704f0849825f1F8b077deeD8d39). You could also specify your Ethereum Name Service (ENS) domain. A human-readable Ethereum address that you can acquire for a set amount of time is known as an ENS domain. It's analogous to Internet domain names like www.-coingecko.com, which then map to the server's IP address where CoinGecko is hosted.

There are various dashboards available on the market that can track your assets, like Frontier, InstaDApp, MyDeFi, and Zerion. To keep things simple, we'll look at DeFiSnap, one of the more well-known dashboards.

## Step-By-Step Guide To Using Defisnap

Step 1:

Navigate to https://www.defisnap.io

Enter your ENS domain or Ethereum address.

I used defiportal.eth here, but I can also enter 0x358a6c0f7614c44b344381b0699e2397b1483252.

Step 2

You're on the dashboard!

You can view your wallet balance as well as any Defi deposits, debt, and investments.

# 2. Tools to Utilize in DeFi

In this chapter of the guide, you will learn tips and tricks to; becoming your own bank, avoid paying capital gains tax, and how you can take money from your assets without selling it. While of course it sounds good I will also display the caveats involved with each method along with my opinion.

Borrow and Lending

Borrowing and lending in crypto can be very dangerous if you don't understand the mechanics. In crypto there are two methods you can use to borrow funds. The first being through a centralized exchange like BlockFi or Celsius. The second way you can borrow funds is through a Decentralized exchange like compound or Aave.

Two ways to borrow crypto:

1. Through a centralized exchange
2. Through a decentralized exchange

Borrowing Through a Centralized Exchange

Borrowing though a crypto exchange is fairly different from taking a loan through a traditional bank. The concept is unique and gives everybody a chance to take a loan out. Now let me clarify that when you are borrowing in this type of method you are borrowing against yourself which benefits a person if they do not want to sell their assets. Now there are loans that don't require you to have any capital upfront.

So, if you have crypto in your account, you can use that crypto as collateral for a loan. You can use your crypto as collateral and withdraw USD, accessing your crypto value without selling your crypto.

Two types of loans:

1. Collateralized- exchanging your asset for a loan
2. Uncollateralized- A loan without any assets backing it

Why is not having to sell your crypto important? Well, if you believe that your investments will go up in price over time, you may not want to sell them before they reach that maturity. Also, you don't have to pay capital gains tax on that money since it is a loan.

In a traditional loan if you miss a payment, your credit score is impacted. There are no credit scores involved in a DeFi loan.

Instead, when you borrow from yourself there are two things that can happen. The first being you can simply pay back the loan in agreed upon terms. Now if you miss a payment, you are charged more in interest. The second thing that can happen is your asset that you Over-collateralized on can get liquidated.

Being liquidated can happen in two ways;

1. Not paying the loan back in agreed upon terms
2. 80% LTV

LTV stands for **Loan to Value**. So, if your loan reaches 80% the value of your asset than your asset will be liquidated.

In most cases you can only borrow 50% of your USD value in btc (Each exchange is different).

Example:

You decide that you want to borrow $1000 worth of your bitcoin. Meaning your bitcoin USD value must be at least $2000. So, to be liquidated your LTV has to be 80%.

LTV (%) = Loan Amount/Value of collateral

So, let's say hypothetically that the value of that $2000 drops to $1200 because the price of bitcoin falls, you would become liquidated. The equation would look as follows:

$$\frac{\text{Loan amount}\$1000}{\text{Value of Collateral }\$1200} \text{x}100 = 83.3\%\text{LTV}$$

In order to not become liquidated when your LTV goes above 80% you must pay down the loan amount. So, using the example above if the value of your collateral is $1200 you want to pay your loan amount down to $500 to keep that 50%LTV.

LTV levels:

50%- safe

65%- you'll begin to get warning messages by the broker

70%- you would begin getting margin calls from this point you would have 72 hours to pay down loan.

80%- automatic liquidation

Cryptocurrencies are very volatile, so you want to be very cautious and always monitor your LTV levels.

## Lending Through a Centralized Exchange

This method is comparable to a savings account. I have seen platforms paying up to 9% in interest. Now it is variable, and you can check which platforms has the best rates with the link below.

Linkà https://loanscan.io/

We now understand how traditional banks truly work. Remember when you hold your money in a savings account, they do not lend it out, instead they balance their books with it so they can leverage more debt from the federal reserve.

The thought you had before about traditional banks lending your money out holds true in a centralized crypto exchange. In the beginning of the book, I promised I'd teach you how to become your own bank this isn't it. We are getting there this method just teaches you that you can utilize a smarter way of saving.

While both lending and borrow through an exchange sounds appetizing, I want to mention that you have to give custodian of your coins away. I have said it many times but, I am going to highlight it again **NOT YOUR KEYS NOT YOUR COINS!⚠** Using an exchange in any kind of way with crypto goes against the entire purpose of why crypto was invented. I am personally not a fan of this method and I do not use it, but while that is my opinion the facts are there, and the choice is yours. I want you to know so you can make an educational decision on how you handle your money. Read on and I will teach the methods I use.

Decentralized Lending and Borrow

Allows users to become lenders or borrowers in a completely decentralized way. Instead of giving your information to an exchange, DeFi protocols such as Aave and Compound run smart contracts on the Ethereum blockchain. These types of tokens operate by creating money markets. Users can choose which ever money market they want to lend their money to and start receiving interest right away (commonly known as yield farming). Now lending in this method works a lot different than lending through a CEX. Remember DEX's do not use order books they use AMM and the formula for AMM is x*y=k. So, when you lend to DEX's you lend token A (x) and Token B (y) which equals the amount of liquidity you are providing (k) as a constant. The interest you receive is not in dollars or in the pair you supplied, instead it is in the native token of the protocol you are lending in.

Example:

In this example we will use the liquidity pool LAZIO-BNB which is offering an APR of 138.5%, which sounds very attractive. How it works is you supply token A- LAZIO and token B-BNB which in return gives you interest in the native protocol which is Pancakes token

CAKE. Now the cavate to this method is the effect of impermanent loss. Impermanent loss happens when the price ratio of the deposited tokens changes. Since the liquidity you provided is a constant if the price of the tokens you supply increases or decreases your liquidity pool is at a loss unless either the price reverts back, or you receive enough in fees to make up that loss. If you decide to withdraw the funds at a loss, then that loss becomes a permanent loss.

On the borrowing side borrowers choose to take collateralized loans out, flash loans or any other service that specific protocols offers. The interest that lenders receive and the interest that borrowers pay are determined by the overall ratio between supplied and borrowed tokens. The interest is calculated per Ethereum block (Ethereum block time usually 13 seconds), so interest rates fluctuate at a very fast rate.

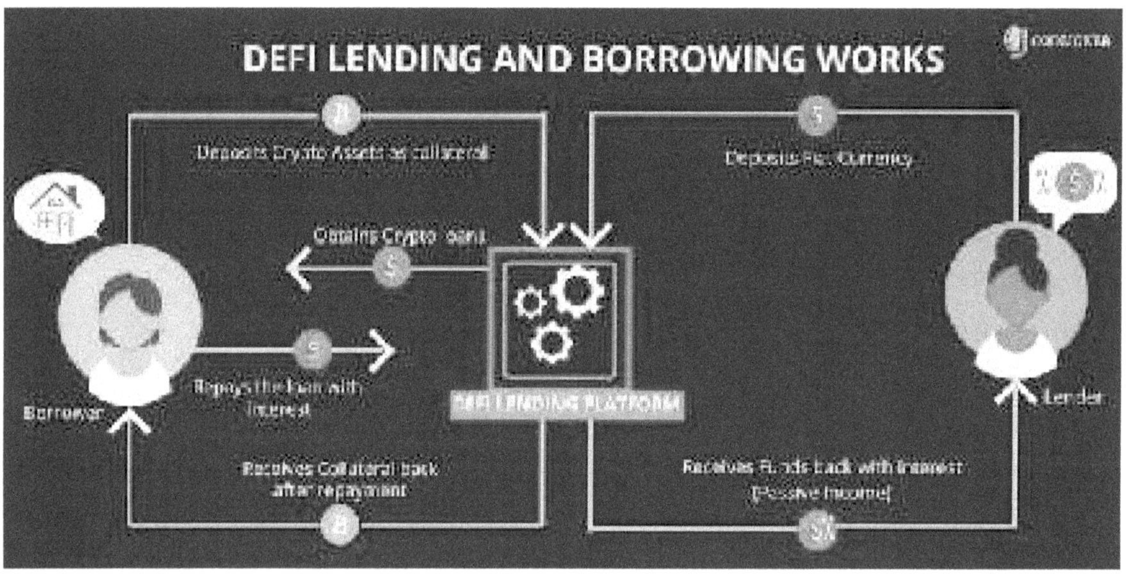


The liquidation process works the exact same as crypto exchanges use them. Some tokens have slightly different parameters for their LTV and liquidation levels. Below shows a chart on each protocol:

**Liquidation stats for different protocols (with ETH as collateral)**

| Protocol | MaterDAO | Compound | Aave |
|---|---|---|---|
| Minimum collateralization ratio | 150% | 133% | 133% |
| Maximum loan-to-value | 66.70% | 75% | 75% |
| Liquidation point (Min.coll.ratio) | <150% | <133% | <125 |
| Liquidation point (LTV) | >66.70% | >75% | >80% |
| Liquidation factor | 1 | 0.5 | 0.5 |
| Liquidation penalty | 13% | 8% | 5% |

Most people borrow in a decentralized token to avoid paying taxes on their gains and not give up custodian to their coins.

The next tool mentioned is what I utilize to earn passive income. This protocol allows me to gain price appreciation and earn inflation from newly minted coins like Bitcoin miners do. It is the token that did a 1,000,000% gain in under two years. Sounds too good to be true? Go check the charts. It is an unbelievable financial instrument running on the block chain.

## HEX Token

Hex is like a certificate of deposit (CD) that is run on the blockchain. Its game theory can be confusing but is superior and will shock you once you understand it. Hex is a token build on the Ethereum blockchain. Hex uses a staking consensus mechanism that allows anyone to stake their coins. When a person stakes their coins, they can lock them up to 15 years (I have stakes locked up for that long). When you lock your coins up, they burn off the market and you receive what's called T-shares or B-shares depending how much you lock and for how long. Those shares are your money printers, so every day at 8pm EST each T-share you have gives you on average 5.74 hex. That hex you receive is the newly minted inflation.

Example:

You lock your money up for 7 years and receive 15 T-shares and the price of hex is $1. Everyday you make 86.1 hex. Convert that to dollars every week your making $602.

15(T-shares) x 5.74 (Inflation)= 86.1 hex * 7 days * $1

= $602 per week.

Now as time goes on the price of hex continues to rise so your money will begin to compound at a very rapid rate.

So, you receive additional hex everyday plus price appreciation when the price is up.

People who stake their money hold the price up and people who hold their bags liquid get diluted because the stakers are receiving all the inflation. The average stake length at the time of this writing is 5.74 years.

Anybody who stakes their coins and doesn't serve out half their stake time will get penalized and half that penalty will go to the origin address (OA) and the other half will go to the staker class.

The price of 1- T-share a year ago was .60 cents, today it is over $9,000! The T-share rate only goes up and to the rate which causes the hex price to only go up and to the right.

Hex is an amazing asset if you want to become your own bank! T-shares are money printers and get you paid every day.

Linkà Hex.com

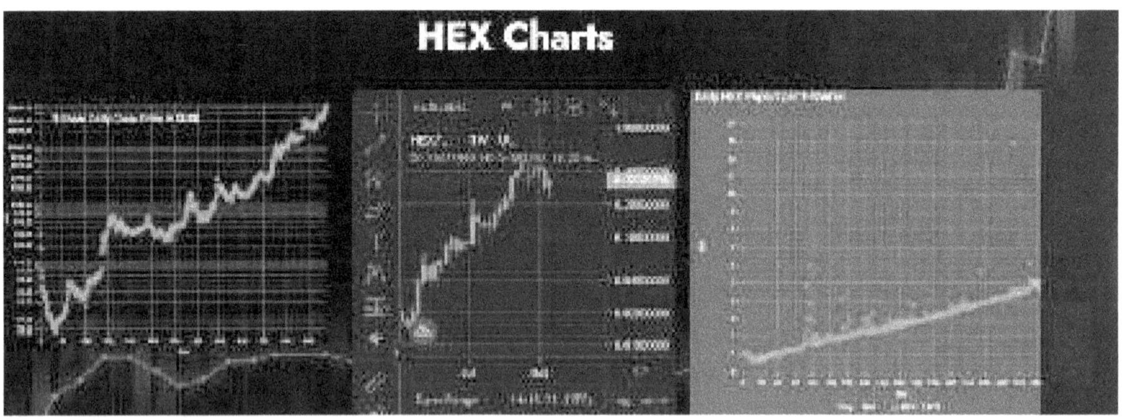


Up and to the right!

# 3. Decentralized Exchanges

Decentralized exchanges, also referred to as DEXs, are peer-to-peer markets where crypto investors conduct transactions without entrusting their assets to an intermediary. Such transactions are made possible via smart contracts, which are self-controlling contracts written in code.

DEXs were developed to eliminate the need for any authority to supervise and allow deals inside a given exchange. Peer-to-peer (P2P) cryptocurrency trading is possible on decentralized exchanges. Peer-to-peer refers to a cryptocurrency marketplace that connects buyers and sellers. They are often non-custodial, meaning that participants retain control over their wallet's private keys. Participants may access their cryptocurrency via a private key, which is a kind of sophisticated encryption. After authenticating into the decentralized exchange with their private key, participants may instantly see their cryptocurrency balances. They will not be needed to provide any personal details or addresses, which is ideal for those who value their privacy.

How DEXs Work

All trade induces a transaction cost in addition to the trading fee since DEXs are built on top of blockchain technology that allows smart contracts and where participants maintain custody of their assets. To use decentralized exchanges, traders engage with smart contracts on the blockchain network.

Automated market makers (AMM), Order books DEXs, and DEX aggregators are the primary forms of DEXs. All of them employ smart contracts to enable participants to trade freely with one another. The early DEXs utilized order books that were comparable to those used by centralized exchanges.

Automated Market Makers (AMMs)

An automated market maker (AMM) system based on smart contracts was developed to address the liquidity issue.

These AMMs use blockchain oracles, which are blockchain-supported services that offer data from exchanges and other networks to establish the price of traded assets. Rather than matching buy and sell orders, these DEXs' smart contracts employ liquidity pools, which are pre-funded pools of assets.

Other participants finance the pools, and they are then subject to the transaction fees charged by the system for implementing transactions on that pair. To earn income on their crypto assets, these liquidity providers must deposit an equal amount of all assets in the trading pair. A process referred to as liquidity mining. If they try to deposit more of an asset than another, the smart contract that runs the pool invalidates the transaction.

Traders can utilize liquidity pools to implement orders or get interest without needing permission or trust. Because the AMM concept has a disadvantage when there isn't sufficient liquidity, these exchanges are frequently rated based on the amount of cash held in their smart contracts, known as total value locked (TVL).

## Order Book DEXs

Order books keep track of all open purchase and sell orders for certain asset pairs. Purchase orders show a trader's willingness to purchase or bid for an asset at a specified price, while sell orders show an investor's willingness to sell or ask for the item in question at a given price. The size of the order book and the market price on the exchange is determined by the gap between these values.

There are two forms of order book DEXs. They are on-chain order books and off-chain order books. Open order information is frequently held on-chain by DEXs that employ order books, while participants' money stays in their wallets. Investors on these exchanges could leverage their holdings by borrowing money from lenders on the site. Leveraged trading improves a trade's earning potential while equally increasing the danger of liquidation. It boosts the size of the position with borrowed money that must be returned even if the investors lose their stake.

On the other hand, DEX platforms that keep their order books off the blockchain simply execute orders on the blockchain to provide traders with the advantages of centralized exchanges. Exchanges can save money and time by using off-chain order books to ensure that deals are performed at the prices that participants want.

These exchanges equally enable participants to lend their cash to other investors to provide leveraged trading opportunities. Loaned money accrue interest with time and is protected by the exchange's liquidation process, which ensures that lenders are compensated even if investors lose theirs.

It's worth noting that order book DEXs frequently have liquidity difficulties. Traders generally adhere to centralized platforms as they are contending with centralized exchanges and pay extra expenses due to the fees needed to transact on-chain. While decentralized exchanges with off-chain order books decrease these expenses, the requirement to deposit cash in smart contracts introduces smart contract-related vulnerabilities.

## DEX aggregators

To deal with liquidity issues, DEX aggregators employ a variety of protocols and methods. These platforms effectively pool liquidity from many decentralized exchanges to reduce slippage on big orders, reduce swap fees and token prices, and provide traders with a better price in the shortest amount of time.

DEX aggregators' other major aims are to protect participants from the price effect and reduce the chance of unsuccessful transactions. Certain DEX aggregators additionally leverage liquidity from centralized systems to give a better user experience, all while staying non-custodial through the usage of specialized centralized exchange integrations.

## DYdX

Although dYdX is restricted basically as a trading platform, it is among the most sophisticated as an open, trustless, and non-custodial platform. Fundamental trading between three simple assets (ETH, DAI, and USDC), lending funds to earn interest, and major types of margin trading (isolated margin trading and cross margin trading) are presently available on the platform. These are basic instruments for a seasoned trader, but they represent a big step forward for the DeFi market.

dYdX closes deals on the blockchain network but employs an off-chain matching algorithm to provide the same implementation speeds as centralized exchanges while maintaining the security of non-custodial assets.

How it Works

Everybody engages in one "universal lending pool," rather than separate borrowers and lenders offering and receiving loan proposals. Every asset has its lending pool, which is handled by smart contracts, allowing for instant withdrawals, borrowing, and lending without necessarily waiting for matches or adequate money. The interest rates of any asset are determined by the interplay between borrowers and lenders–demand and supply.

Margin Trading

dYdX enables margin trading in conjunction with spot trading (changing one digital token to another), allowing cryptocurrency investors to perform more complex trading methods.

Margin trading, equally referred to as leveraged trading, enables traders to take greater holdings by borrowing money from a third party. Not only does this enable expert traders to increase their trading earnings (and losses!), but it equally allows regular traders to take greater holdings with a smaller amount of initial cash.

Example:

If you're optimistic about Ethereum, you might use a $1,000 initial margin to enter a 5x leveraged trade on ETH/USDC. In that situation, you'd have $5,000 worth of ETH/USDC exposure. If the price increased by 10%, the position would be increased by $500 (rather than just $100), giving you a 50% return on your investment if you closed it out at that time.

If the bullish conviction is incorrect and the price of ETH falls by $10 against USDC, the worth of the $1000 5x leveraged position will be reduced to $500. A 50% drop in value.

All you have to do to begin trading on dYdX is link your Ethereum wallet. The Trust Wallet in-app DApp Browser is the easiest method to achieve this on mobile. You may also use WalletConnect to access the web-supported edition of dYdX.

Traders can also use margin trading to short assets they anticipate will fail. Short selling an asset entails borrowing it to sell it and then purchasing it back later (ideally at a lower price) to benefit whenever the asset's value declines.

If Ethereum's bearish anticipates the cryptocurrency's price will fall in the following days, they may utilize dYdX to short ETH against USDC or DAI (with up to 5x leverage).

How to Make Money with dYdX

If you've ever searched through aggregators of DeFi loan rates, you've probably come across dYdX. Because the platform is decentralized, participants may borrow and lend Ethereum-supported assets.

dYdX makes it easier to earn interest on digital assets than any other DeFi protocol. It's straightforward. You will begin to receive interest immediately after you deposit cash into the platform on the 'Balances' tab. That's all there is to it! And every minute that your dollars are stored in the platform, you will receive interest.

Borrowing (mainly margin traders) on the platform pays interest on stored assets. Because dYdX allows only collateral-based borrowing, if borrowers fail to repay or their collateral value falls below a set limit, their collateral is instantly liquidated to safeguard lenders.

dYdX has reproduced the famous cryptocurrency derivatives offering from prominent centralized exchanges like Bitfinex and BitMEX in a safe, transparent, and trustless manner, rendering it better than its centralized counterparts in many respects.

# Uniswap

Uniswap is an Ethereum platform for trading ERC20 tokens. Uniswap, unlike other exchanges, is meant to be a public good—a means for the public to trade tokens without paying platform fees or dealing with intermediaries. Uniswap also utilizes basic arithmetic and pools of tokens and ETH to accomplish the same function as conventional exchanges that connect buyers and sellers to establish prices and conduct transactions.

## How It Work

In comparison to centralized exchanges, the Uniswap platform takes a unique approach. Its open-source program is based on the Ethereum network, and it enables participants to trade ERC-20 tokens without the involvement of a third party. This can assist in decreasing expenses while also resolving certain tricky censorship concerns.

Without the use of an order book, liquidity providers play a critical role in making things happen. Anybody can participate in these liquidity pools by contributing the equal value of two tokens, like ETH and stablecoins like USDT or DAI. They'll earn liquidity pool tokens in return, which they may spend on other decentralized applications. This equally assures that they will be able to receive their donation at any moment.

When participants conduct a swap using a trading pair, they are charged transaction fees, with a part of this going to the liquidity provider according to the pool tokens they possess.

Uniswap pools are based on the equation "x * y = k.*."

Here, x might be ETH, y could be USDT, and k could be the result of multiplying x and y to find the pool's total liquidity. Constant product market makers — smart contracts that store liquidity pools — assume that k must always be fixed.

Assume that somebody buys ETH in exchange for USDT via a liquidity pool. As a result of this trade, there will be less ETH in the liquidity pool and more USDT.

Somebody who buys ETH from a liquidity pool in return for USDT will adjust the balance between the assets in this transaction pair, raising the price of ETH while lowering the price of USDT. In bigger liquidity pools, this slippage is typically less evident.

Uniswap's major benefits are its ease of use compared to other DEXs and the fact that traders are no longer accountable for supplying liquidity.

## How Uniswap Tokens are Created

The donor gets a "pool token," which is also an ERC20 token, anytime fresh ETH/ERC20 tokens are given to a Uniswap liquidity pool.

When money is placed into the pool, pool tokens are produced, and like an ERC20 token, they may be freely traded, transferred, and utilized in other Dapps. The pool tokens are burnt or destroyed when money is recovered. Every pool token reflects a participant's portion of the pool's overall assets as well as their portion of the pool's 0.3 percent transaction fee.

How to Make Your First Uniswap Trade

You may buy ether (ETH) and any of the hundreds of ERC20 tokens offered by the platform using Uniswap.

To do so, you'll need enough ETH in your account to cover any transaction costs and something to exchange for the ERC20 token you desire. This may be ETH or another ERC20 token. If you want to trade USD Coin (USDC) for UNI, for instance, you'll require USDC in the wallet as well as enough ether to pay the trading fee.

We'll go through how to buy some UNI tokens with ETH and perform your first transaction on Uniswap.

- Step 1: Go to the Uniswap exchange site.

Select the ‘Connect to a wallet' option in the top right corner, then log in with the wallet you want to transact with. A MetaMask, WalletConnect, Coinbase Wallet, Fortmatic, or Portis Wallet may be used.

We'll use a MetaMask wallet to log in for this explanation.

- Step 2: The transaction page will display once you've logged in.

Choose the token you like to swap for the other token you want in the top area. You may go with ETH. Look for the token you want to buy in the bottom area, or choose it from the drop-down option, in this instance UNI.

- Step 3: You're finally set to place your order.

You may enter a number in the top area to indicate what you like to spend or a number in the bottom area to indicate what you want to purchase.

Let's assume we acquire 0.1 ETH worth of UNI tokens in our illustration.

- Step 4: At the bottom of the order menu, you'll find an estimate of what you'll get.

Hit the 'Swap' option when you're satisfied with the results. The wallet click would then ask you to authorize the transaction and, if necessary, change the fees to a level that is most convenient for you.

Approve the transaction once you're set, and it'll be executed. The tokens will display in the ERC20 wallet after this is completed.

- Next Steps

There are many choices for advanced users after you've made your first transaction on Uniswap. Because Uniswap is an open smart contract platform, a variety of front-end user interfaces have already been developed. InstaDApp, for instance, enables you to deposit money into Uniswap pools without utilizing the regular Uniswap user interface.

Participants can add funds to Uniswap pools using only ETH rather than ETH and another token utilizing interfaces like Zapper.fi. Easy, one-click options for acquiring pool tokens in conjunction with bZx token schemes are available through the interface.

# Balancer

Balancer is a decentralized exchange that uses an automated market maker (AMM) and liquidity pools. It is based on the Ethereum network. It allows participants to trade cryptos and receive interest on their unused crypto holdings.

Balancer participants can trade ERC-20 assets without depending on a centralized body by using liquidity pools. They may also offer liquidity in exchange for a portion of the trading fees. Balancer distinguishes itself from the competition by allowing customers to build their private liquidity pools or pools with more than two cryptos. Balancer provides several incentives to enhance liquidity on the Balancer Protocol in the long run.

## Balancer token (BAL)

Balancer (BAL) is the Balancer protocol's native governance token. BAL token owners can vote on the protocol's growth. Although the network does not currently have a defined governance structure, token owners can vote on layer two solutions, the installation of Balancer on blockchains other than Ethereum, and fee adjustments at the protocol level.

## How it Works

The Balancer exchange is an automated market maker (AMM), which implies transactions are settled without traditional order books. Balancer pools that are liquidity pools made up of 2 to 8 cryptos are used instead. These offer the liquidity that investors want. The AMM utilizes the percentage of tokens inside a liquidity pool to establish exchange rates. Smart contracts are used to accomplish exchanges.

Whenever a new Balancer pool is formed, the developer determines the token ratio in the pool. For example, if a pool contains Tether, Ether, and wBTC, the ratios might be adjusted to 25 percent, 25 percent, and 50 percent, respectively. When compared to Tether and Ether, there would be twice the amount of wBTC.

When a trader utilizes a liquidity pool to execute a transaction, the liquidity pool is rebalanced. Any imbalances in the pool might provide traders with arbitrage possibilities. The arbitrage trader makes money by taking advantage of the pool's imbalance compared to the actual-world market exchange rate. This arbitrage mechanism constantly rebalances the liquidity pool. However, fees are still collected from liquidity providers and individuals who formed the liquidity pool.

## Balancer Pools

To accommodate varied risk appetites, Balancer provides two forms of pools: public pools and private pools. By contributing digital assets to public pools, anybody may offer liquidity to Balancer. These pools' settings are established before they go live and cannot be altered, even by the pool's creators. Stockholders that want to earn fees from their holdings might consider joining a public pool.

Private liquidity pools are those in which only the creator can add or remove assets. The developer also adjusted other pool criteria, such as allowed assets, fees, and weightings.

How to trade on Balancer

A participant will need access to cryptos through a Web 3.0 digital wallet like MetaMask before transacting on the Balancer platform. MetaMask is a browser plugin that serves as a link between the digital asset holdings and decentralized apps like Balancer.

To trade on Balancer, follow these steps:

- Balancer. Log onto the Balancer platform.
- Link your wallet. Link your Web 3.0 digital wallet, such as MetaMask
- Decide on a crypto. Select the crypto you want to sell or purchase from the dropdown set of possible tokens. You may accomplish this by entering the token's name, address, or symbol.
- Fill in the amount. Once you've made your choice, you'll need to input the quantity of crypto you want to trade. After filtering across relevant pools carrying the tokens required, Balancer will offer you the best potential price as you start to input the "token to sell" amount.
- Confirm. On your MetaMask or Web 3.0 digital wallet, click "Swap" and complete the transaction. The crypto sold will be withdrawn from the digital wallet when the transaction is completed on the Ethereum network, and the crypto acquired will be added.

# 4. Understanding Decentralization Myths

The people who plagiarize stuff on the internet, gaining control of all the networks and tools, put forward on their own the minor details of the problem that are included in the website that they plunder. Even though their viewpoint assures more but creates the following of a growing number of opponents. As people were made aware of Nakamoto's plans, splinter groups resembling an anemone were laid by Nakamoto, which resulted in the mass spread of cryptocurrencies & blockchains everywhere. It would have been an impeccable camouflage (the 2014 ICO Boom) for the attempt of the group at a coup on the United States, but failed when the boon of the industry was doubted as treachery by the US and Cicada stayed legally latent.

Even though I am not aware of the true initiative of Cicada but what I do know is that Cicada and Henrici are inclined to question in contradiction the ways of peace established. Similarly, Nakamoto questioned against the established ways of finance. With Nakamoto's paper began the Decentralized myth in cryptocurrency which meant that the government controlling the worth of value wouldn't be good. Like stocks, the governmental regulations do not determine the value of Bitcoin but instead, it gets its value from the values of its enterprise.

Nakamoto, whose identity nobody knows, through his name into the woodworks of an enterprise. Hypothetically an enterprise talking to a government. In order to control law enforcement high crime subsidies, in 2005 the United States was on the outlook for financial services. President Bush was counseled by his advisors to take notice of the usefulness of the storage of the value Bitcoin possessed, but it was a small-scale company and hence it didn't fit the desires of the American public.

The Homeland Security Act's Byrne Justice Assistance Grant was the winner of the competition for law enforcement. Robert Byrne of VA who was an ambulance chaser started this and it has been the hole in the bowl leaking America's funding. The first payment was made by the grant in 2006 with $6 billion being paid to the 17 states with peaking crime rates. The following year our Treasury secretary and a few of his pals start price-fixing credit ratings for promissory notes.

His action is conceivable only if the Nakamoto paper belittles governments and the funding of high crime states for having high crime are all about money, which they were. This action ended up collapsing three industries i.e., Banking, Housing, and Automobiles. Successively, there was a scarcity of jobs in not only America but the world too.

Satoshi Nakamoto went underground and was never heard from again. Further calamity was caused in America as the money used to subsidize law enforcement high-crime grants could not be used to fortify banks, so naturally, America had to ask for money. The promoting businesses, who were held accountable for this catastrophe received money, which resulted in businesses coming up and discovering new ways to fund the catastrophe (Oil Surplus) to accept bailout similar to the promoting businesses. All those who actually contributed to this catastrophe would come across a calamity from their own business plans but Bitcoin would prove to be a savior for a few.

2008 has Bitcoin catch traction with the introduction of Reddit and 4Chan. This turned Bitcoin into a cryptocurrency used to gamble, buy chat room game collectibles, buy NFTs, which was soon followed with it being assumed "real-world" value with the initial "transaction" when for 10,000 Bitcoin, two large Pizzas were bought from Papa Johns. Which was followed by the big leagues as the designer NFTs and the Pizza story turned into a bizarre art and costly electronics out of China. The Casinos of the Chinese Islands were told that they needed to be a part of the act, so they built an online casino that only accepted Bitcoin

At present, Decentralized Autonomous Organization (DAO) has the ownership of numerous cryptocurrencies of their own, not Bitcoin. Even though loyalty is centralized, Bitcoin is still used at the Casinos for loyalty tokens. Their point is that they are their own business and it didn't take long to understand that, nor did it matter.

The significant concept of the decentralized myth is Loyalty. Initially sold as a loyalty token Bitcoin became the target of attempted plagiarism which ended up stealing a 99% share of the market awareness. It was sheer luck that the remaining 1% turned into such a strong network of finance which was equivalent in wealth to the economy of Venezuela, the 6th largest economy in the world. The aggressive attempt certainly had a windfall, and market analysis anticipates regulation to end the oppression and create a strategy for mass adoption.

Bitcoin is not Satoshi Nakamoto as a BX in Thailand, as proved by regulatory issues. Policies like AML/KYC, introduced by governments to capture Satoshi Nakamoto were utilized Bitcoin's home exchange. Additionally, determining projects such as Civic by Roger, Ver, or Pavo by IBM, within cryptocurrency seek to do business with governments. Laws of all the top 10 nations with well-developed economies permit the fair trade of cryptocurrency under-regulated measures which is the description of regulated by a central bank.

The dominant philosophy of the decentralized myth that started with the publishing of the Satoshi Nakamoto paper was to upkeep misconduct by derestricting currency. The weakness was that the governments have money as well.

Though the decentralized myth did give us some positive outcomes. Firstly, the elucidation of how transaction processing was crowdsourced by Bitcoin through publicly outsourcing mining algorithms procreated the concept of crowdsourcing. Crowd-funding was acclaimed as a harmless method of finance while the Initial Coin Offerings (ICOs) were thought of as evil.

$200 million was gathered by the ICO market in the year 2017, which was its peak time. But unfortunately, it also brought a lot of fraud and scams. Out of all the ICOs that collected the money barely half of them started doing business. Since it was free money, there were no accountabilities if you didn't raise enough. It wasn't expected for the cryptocurrency to go any farther than video games and the internet unless it had a blockchain.

2018 was the revolutionary year because this was the time when every project was unexpectedly in need of a real-world application. Cryptocurrency and Bitcoin was no longer just a token for video games but instead, it was an entire financial instrument. The products related to agriculture presently had validation of freshness and were followed by augmented reality games and artificial intelligence.

2019 witnessed the dirty business of manipulation and deregulation. Manipulation is all about setting up others just so your chances are better. In cryptocurrency, manipulation was all about the fights regarding the decentralized myth with the biggest question being about mass adoption. "Bitcoin Purists" were in favor of upholding the instability of the currency to keep the hedging long, while finance-minded organizations were in favor of stabilizing the currency. The gamers and coders and had the power to diverge the steadiness and ensure volatility. The BCC fork was more of an inspiration to Congress for needing a diverse structure for the tax for a few businesses. So, we can say that deregulation of the cryptocurrency created more users in a way. This is something that would flame the arguments that shaped the modern cryptocurrency exchange.

Now according to the AML/KYC policies, the US has to tax structures for Bitcoin businesses who envisioned the 'deregulation' as the position the industry would stand on going into the next decade, and over 34,000 crypto exchanges. To the public eye, the word decentralized has developed into an occurrence that is greater than cryptocurrency... crowdsourcing.

But crowdsourcing is only one of the concepts of decentralization. The deleterious aspect that was discovered by the myth has both good and bad consequences. On one hand, crime is being lured into the industry. Cryptocurrency is seen by many as a way out of an undesirable lifecycle, while according to those in finance who are wise, the myth is drafting criminals for an overthrow plot, which is similar to the chance taken by Pro-Trump demonstrators when attacking the capital.

The only real danger posed by the myth was that it was supposed to target governments so that companies like General Motors could protest against the government until being given a bailout. All in all, decentralization took on more significance than the threat posed on the world by Lee Iacocca. Lee Iacocca wanted to build every car driven and own every business. And he would go to any limits to achieve his aim and nothing would stop him to accomplish what he wished for and wanted, not even a forged racial identity.

Blockchain is not a threat:

Media and pundits alike are inspired by cryptocurrencies and their fundamental technology – the blockchain.

Since the technological setup of the blockchain is complex and would confuse not only the average reader but the crypto-lovers too, they might not be acquainted with the financial terminology and payment infrastructure.

Due to this unfamiliarity, many persistent myths have been born that have reinforced most blockchain discussions. Most of these myths are either wrong or too one-dimensional and, thus they cloud the aptitude of decision-makers to make judgments and ability to reach conclusions.

There are three tangled assumptions that jointly fuel the argument regarding blockchain technology breaking banks.

Myth 1: "Open blockchains rather than closed will power tomorrow's economy"

The main reason for the spread of blockchain technology was the excitement and enthusiasm of people about getting rid of banks. When Bitcoin was created in 2008, due to the financial crisis the following of blockchain technology grew rapidly. A solution to the financial system run by big financers was presented in the form of the technical arrangement of Bitcoin and its decentralized nature it has. Although it was later seen that decentralization was not mandatory for a blockchain.

There are two general major blockchain setups:

- Centralized or "closed"
- Decentralized or "open"

Every blockchain system has a system of multiple nodes to upkeep a ledger instead of having a middleman. This shows that the blockchain system is distributed. In decentralized ("open") no node is advantaged over the others by the algorithm. On the contrary, in centralized ("closed") chains some nodes are given more weightage than others.

In a decentralized blockchain- like Bitcoin, where everybody can participate in verifying transactions and each node carries the same weight.

Though, there is not always a precise discrepancy. In Ripple, one out of the three major crypto coins, the degree of centralization is still debated and disputed upon within the industry. The case with it as a blockchain is similar, the transactions that are recorded are not piled up as blocks, instead, they look like a large ledger. So the question arises, why does this distinction matter?

There are many limitations to the original, decentralized model. Some of these include the unmaintainable energy-consumption, the unapproachable necessary scale, the usability a pain, and regulation a thing to be circumvented by design, financial transactions taking far too long, moreover the currency problems faced by crypto-coins and this can lead us to understand the cynicism of many officials. All these weaknesses and limitations could have been eliminated in the centralized blockchains as the majority of the financial institutions regard it as the model of choice.

Despite all this why is the hype around the open blockchain? This technological disagreement is indicative of a deep ideological split at the center of the blockchain debate. On one side, there are officials of the banking and payments world, whereas on the other side what we see is an unusual coalition of crypto-evangelists, anarcho-libertarians, entrepreneurs, and fraudsters who are set for the commotion. The concluding group characterizes the founders and early adopters of the blockchain and still carries substantial weight in determining public debate about it. What they see in the blockchain is the means to bring down any kind of trusted institution which according to them is only possible with truly decentralized applications.

Myth 2: "With the success of the blockchain comes the downfall of banks"

Bearing in mind the background of primary investors of crypto, it is possibly conventional that banks are announced to be the first targets of the blockchain.

As stated, however, the model with at least some kind of centralization will be the winning model. This already cries out for a dealer of trust, implying that banks will be part of the equation. And even if the algorithm is completely decentralized there will still be some institutions that would need to handle data and rights to access pre or post a transaction. Bitcoins also have such institutions which are exchanges, you can trade, buy or sell bitcoin on these exchanges. Even bitcoins need institutions such as exchanges where you can buy and sell them.

Just a small part of the banks' value chain is comprised of payments. Even if cryptocurrencies succeeded to displace banks from moving value, what they wouldn't be able to do is replace them in providing everlasting and steady storage of value. Neither could the supplying of finances work devoid of financial institutions. Blockchains do not break into the banks, but the banks can break into markets so they can accept the digital standard.

Myth 3: "FinTechs are the banks' main challenge"

This third myth impeccably merges in with the first two. Decentralization, as opposed to the very nature of banks, lays the foundation for their fall and therefore, there also needs to be an immaculate challenger to push them from their throne.

The young and nimble FinTechs are responsible for this role. They start anew and can dedicate their entire energy to new products. Dynamic FinTechs can easily follow along any direction that the market takes. It has already happened to retail and hardware-manufacturing, and now it is also happening to finance?

The real reason why these examples are so noticeable is that they are the exclusion rather than the rule. Studies show that an industry structure is missed up not only due to greenfield competition, but the majority of the time it is due to incumbents or by market recruits prevailing in other industries. As a rule, new applicants lack the scale, financial muscle, and brand awareness. Typically, it takes longer to build those up than to guide mandatory supertankers into the winning direction.

Paypal is an example that is frequently mentioned when showing that banking is not immune to modernization. Dissimilar from Visa or Mastercard, it is not a result of banking collaboration, nevertheless, it has hitherto become the chief online payment system in North America. It comprises over 354 billion USD in payment volume internationally. The amount of active user accounts on Paypal has surpassed 200 million. But Paypal surrounds itself around the currently existing system. It does not succeed in credit cards or bank accounts but instead supplements them. Blockchain start-ups are an entirely different tale. Banks have realized long ago that the technology will aid them in saving a lot of money in the back-end. Innumerable initiatives, attainments, and blockchain labs are evidence of this. They will not be caught slumbering again.

And finally, one critical question rests: Do FinTechs really want to relocate the existing incumbents? Most mission statements definitely read as if this is the goal, yet in a study, 75.5% of all FinTechs announce that partnering with a recognized firm is their main goal. An intention might be that now the majority of the start-up blockchains are driven by obligatory investment like Veem took $25 million from cooperation run by Goldman Sachs.

The perseverance of these three myths definitely has sustained the interest in blockchain technology. These myths are unpretentious, speak to an engaged target group, and can be supported with carefully selected attention-grabbing examples. Believing them gullibly might end up costing you actual money – regardless of the fact if you are bearing in mind buying a crypto-coin or as a corporate decision-maker you anticipate financing original infrastructure.

Due to its mass of mechanisms and the resulting fuzziness, even more, fallacies surround blockchain technology. To devise a longstanding plan for blockchain that will not be directed by the latest news items, it is obligatory to clear those up.

# 5. How to enter DeFi?

In order to get into DeFi investments, first we need to know some tools where to buy cryptocurrencies. These are the three main ones, let's know their advantages and disadvantages.

## Binance

If you don't have an account yet, sign up from the following affiliate link and you'll enjoy 10% off **trading** fees for life:

https://www.binance.com/es/register?ref=QR0YPYFC

This is a platform for exchanging cryptocurrencies, is one of the most users in the world. it was launched in July 2017. It has an ICO to finance the development of the Exchange. This allows the platform not to depend on venture capital companies, being funded by the community.

Binance launched its ICO on July 3 and put up for sale 100 million ERC20 tokens called BNB (Binance Coin). It lasted just 3 minutes and managed to raise $15 million. 11 days after launching the ICO the Exchange was already available.

There were many registered users after the launch, it generated some access problems due to the large volume of users. Today it is valued at more than two billion dollars.

If we look at the Binance menu we find a series of options for each of its tasks:

- Exchange: to exchange cryptocurrencies, where real-time analysis of the market will appear.
- Academy: cryptocurrency education. Courses, tutorials and more on the subject.
- BCF: is a **blockchain** charitable foundation. Information about the company's charities and donations.
- Info: has information about cryptocurrencies, such as exchange rates, traded volumes and costs.
- Labs: is an incubator for outstanding **blockchain** projects. This is where the company's team that will develop **blockchain** solutions is located.
- Launch pad: is a platform for users to launch their own tokens.
- Research: has information about the company, about mission, tasks and who they are.
- Trust wallet: is an official cryptocurrency wallet.

It also has another series of folding menus on the upper right side. There a number of options appear:

- Funds: deposits, withdrawals, balances, withdrawal and deposit histories, and credit card purchases.
- Order management: you have open orders, order history and transaction history.
- Careers: application for studies with the academy.
- Support: information on common problems with users and solutions.
- News: recent publications in the press about the company and other related topics.

After seeing all this, let's look at the advantages and disadvantages of Binance.

**Advantages**

- You can open an account for free.
- You can choose the language in which you want to operate it.
- It is capable of processing one million transactions per second.
- Their fees are low for transactions and withdrawals.
- It has a community rewards program.
- There is security, and confidence.
- Optional Visa card.

**Disadvantages**

- At the beginning the handling can be complicated.
- It has a support that could be tedious.
- You have to go through KYC (Know Your Customer) registration.

Although it may have some disadvantages, when it comes to using it and knowing it, it is one of the best options and therefore one of the most used in the world.

## Bit2Me

If you don't have an account yet, sign up from the following affiliate link and they will give you 5 euros if your first purchase is 100 euros or more:

https://bit2me.com/es/registro?r=GVT-J5S-DE3

Founded in 2014, it specializes in financial technology. It has a great knowledge in **blockchain** technology and cryptocurrencies, helping individuals, **exchanges**, mining **pools**, issuing tokens, investment funds, governments and institutions, trading and managing different digital assets in an optimal way.

It serves as a gateway to frictionless markets, rendering the traditional financial system obsolete. It was created with the vision of transparency and open and efficient financial systems. It supports many initiatives in the DeFi system, interacting with protocols, providing liquidity and participating in networks that encompass decentralized lending, trading and other financial applications.

The entire systems are developed internally by its operators and considers both a technological and commercial enterprise, creating products, processes and tools to change the world, with the goal of enabling frictionless, fair and transparent markets.

Among its functions we can find:

- Cryptocurrency wallet. _
- It has a trading platform. _
- Bit2me Pay._
- Crypto payments can be accepted in the business. _
- It has secure cryptocurrency custody. _
- Tikebit. _
- MasterCard to pay some cryptocurrencies. _
- Exclusive services for clients. _

Bit2Me released its own token called B2M. It's not in all countries yet, you can only use the platform if you reside in: Austria, Belgium, Bulgaria, Croatia, Cyprus, Czech Republic, Denmark, Estonia, Finland, France, Germany, Greece, Hungary, Ireland, Italy, Latvia, Lithuania, Luxembourg, Malta, Netherlands, Poland, Portugal, Romania, Slovakia, Slovenia, Spain, Sweden, UK. Argentina, Bolivia, Brazil, Chile, Colombia, Costa Rica, Dominican Republic, El Salvador, Mexico, Panama, Puerto Rico, Peru and Uruguay. The list is constantly growing so it is a good idea to check if it is already available in any other country you are interested in.

You have to create an account, before trading you have to go through a data validation process. It is a process that you achieve quickly. To be able to use it you need to have set up the profile well, filling in all the data and attaching your ID. It is an important step in this kind of platform.

There are those who do not trust this step, but the truth is that these operations are banking and it is necessary that you have your information here. If you become a millionaire, you can put on a face and then pay taxes like a good citizen. Another feature is that you have recently incorporated in Bit2Me Trade, for people who are new to the world of **trading** or for professionals.

It's not just for buying cryptocurrencies though. It is a team of people who provide knowledge and value to the community. This world is very wide and needs people to clarify all the information. They have their project called Academy, where they provide a lot of valuable information. It is a reliable exchange, although as confident as they are you should not trust your assets to any **exchange**, the good thing is that they share the same opinion. If you invest a lot to save and leave it in an external **wallet**, you should not have the money in the **blockchain**.

The point is to use it to buy with the affiliate link, remember that only for this you will be earning five euros when you make a purchase of one hundred. Then you can decide what to do with the cryptoassets, whether to keep them in the Exchange (which will soon offer **staking** options like the other two **exchanges** we see in this book) or send them to interact with some protocol.

**Advantages**

- Those responsible have faces and names. There is transparency, with a physical office, and there are many **exchanges** that do not. _
- They have customer service in Spanish. It is of high quality or at least they try. They even have a phone number. _
- They are available 24 hours a day, every day of the year. _
- There is a lot of information on their blog, they have tutorials and guides. _
- They have their own wallet. _
- They have a very active YouTube channel with interesting videos for you to learn more. _
- They currently have relevant people in their team. _

Disadvantages

- They are demanding in the verification process. _
- You can't find all the cryptocurrencies on the market to buy, but you can find the most important ones. _
- If you are going to make large investments, commissions may be very high. _

## Coinbase

If you sign up for an account after clicking on the following affiliate link and if you buy or sell more than $100 in the first 180 days, you will receive $10 or the equivalent in another currency for free:

https://www.coinbase.com/join/blzque_ou

It is a great platform that offers you many advantages. Among them, you can see the graphs with the evolution of prices, you can know how the value of the cryptocurrencies you have goes up or down. Let's analyze this platform in detail.

It acts as a digital **wallet**, which means that you can use it to store your cryptocurrencies in a unified place. Think of it like your bank's app, where you can see the amount of cryptocurrencies you have and the value with their evolution. Also, each wallet will also have a unique address with which others can send cryptocurrencies to it, allowing you to receive or make payments with them without having to go through other services.

On the other hand, it is also a trading service, which is known as a cryptocurrency exchange. Here you can link your credit card and make use of the money to buy various cryptos.

With this, you have a service whose operation is very similar to others such as PayPal (something that Binance and Bit2Me do not yet allow) or your bank's app. You can manage them as if it were a stock market app, but instead of speculating on the market, you can do it with the cryptocurrency market.

The company is based in San Francisco, California, was founded in 2012 by Brian Armstrong and Fred Ehrsam. BBVA has been one of the major investors. It has more than 30 million users.

Coinbase charges you commissions when you buy or sell cryptocurrencies, when buying you have a commission of 1.49%, and when selling to convert them into fiat money, the commission is 1%. What it does not have is commission on transfers of assets to other virtual wallets.

To register is very easy, you just need to be of legal age, give the service the name, surname, email and password, you can make use in the account. Then you link another payment method that can be a PayPal account, bank, credit or debit card.

Coinbase can be used on mobile or on the website. You can see the fiat money value of your investments, the evolution of the main cryptos and decide which ones you want to be shown to you, seeing a summary of the outstanding news of the sector. There is a button called Trade, where you can buy, sell or convert cryptocurrencies. In any of the cases before accepting the operation will always appear the commission you have to pay so that everything is clear to you.

You will also see a bar with options like Portfolio, where you can know the status of the assets, seeing the money you have in the various cryptos and the evolution. In Coinbase the information also appears on the home page, and is deliberately in Portfolio.

You also find the Pricing section, where you can see the current status of the assets that allows you to manage Coinbase, both what you have bought and what you haven't bought. It will tell you the current state of the market in general, the value of the assets in real time, how much you have gone up or down with respect to the value of each asset in the last 24 hours.

You also have the settings section where you can add payment methods or make invitations to earn euro balance by getting others to sign up. You can set your local currency or purchase limits, which can be set to an amount of money per day in the steps or to spend without control what you want. You can set a PIN to protect the application, notifications, privacy or email.

**Advantages**

- It is the safest and simplest way to exchange real money for cryptocurrencies. _
- It offers a variety of withdrawal and deposit options. _
- All deposits are insured. _
- It has a multi-signature security level. _
- It has an affiliate program where you can earn 10 euros for every 100 euros invested by your referrals. _

Disadvantages

Here are the negative points you might want to consider:

- Private keys for cryptocurrencies are for the exclusive use of Coinbase, nobody knows them... not even you. _
- The account is constantly monitored for illegalities, if the algorithm detects any irregularities, Coinbase may close your account. _

All platforms are a great option

Although all three platforms studied have their disadvantages, they also have advantages, so all of them are an option for you to trade, all depending on your needs.

Although Binance and Coinbase have financial products that are more or less decentralized compared to what Bit2Me has, these **blockchain** based products allow you to trade and acquire and send them to your Metamask wallet and access the protocols.

Binance and Coinbase have always had a duel for which one is the best, this can be found in many forums around the internet. Both platforms differ in the type of cryptos they accept on the platforms. While the former has a wider portfolio, the latter is more exclusive. You have to look at the usability, since to have a good experience you need to find a platform that allows you to manage investments in a practical way.

Coinbase has some good opinions about its interface, which is very intuitive, compared to Binance which can be a bit overwhelming at first. The former can provide a more straightforward cryptocurrency trading and investment process.

About security, is it safe to leave assets on Binance? Yes, it supports users with two-factor authentication offered by Google Authenticator. It allows transactions and data modifications by entering the password and validating the access code sent by the mobile phone.

Coinbase is no slouch when it comes to security either, every action you take has its own insurance policy. There are funds in external **wallet**, avoiding hacks. So which one is better depends on the strategies you have in trading.

Binance is an attractive option for those who want to trade cryptos at reasonable rates, because in addition to having a lot of options, the commissions are the lowest, although as I said before, it can be complex to use. Although on mobile phone it has a version called Lite that you can enable or disable and make quick trades are so many buttons or menus.

## Wallet

When you buy cryptocurrencies you must have a place to keep them and guard them. You must take care of them, just like when you withdraw money from the ATM. That is why it is important that you have a wallet or wallet and know the types, uses and risks of each one.

Deciding which wallet is best for you depends on the needs you have, each type of wallet is best suited to a specific purpose and personalized profile. Let's take a look at each one:

### Hardware Wallet

Imagine a pendrive, a small device that connects via USB. The validation of the transfer is done by the wallet itself, its use is safe, even on infected devices.

In order to serve a better function, the private address keys, which are like the password, should be stored offline.

### Paper wallets

They are simple, you only need a piece of paper where you write the private key and the public address printed or written. You don't need to leave data online that can be exposed to attacks, avoiding theft or hacking of access to assets.

However, it is important that you do not allow others to have access to the paper, because it allows you to trade your funds.

### Computer Wallets

Bitcoin and other cryptocurrencies have software created to operate as wallets, some of these can be placed on the desktop allowing access to the network. There are more robust ones like Bitcoin Core, which download the entire blockchain to the computer, consuming a lot of space and internet bandwidth.

## Mobile wallets

They allow you to operate anywhere and at any time. Some have options to synchronize with the computer.

When you choose a mobile wallet, you need to verify that the private key is in your possession. So that in case of a problem you can access the funds from another device or wallet.

## Online Wallet

They depend on a company that is responsible for the security of the assets. In order to use them you require registration and credentials, similar to creating an email account.

Among the options you can choose Ripio, where you can see quotes, buy, sell, send and receive cryptos in a fast and secure way.

## How can you choose the best wallet?

There are those who prefer to use hardware wallets to hold assets for a long time, those who want to save them and rest assured that they will not be robbed of their growing capital, for small amounts others use an online wallet.

You can always combine different wallets with different security measures according to the purpose you have with those assets. If you can, I advise you to try various forms of storage so that you can experiment with the one that suits your needs.

## Difference between DeFi 1.0 and DeFi 2.0

Stage 1.0, represented by Uniswap and Sushiswap, demonstrated the powerful subversive capabilities of decentralized finance. The new financial ecology represented by decentralized exchanges is already showing its charm.

There are great results with DeFi 1.0, although also shortcomings, many projects are tokens that want to print money and this without solutions in the distribution of governance tokens and community governance. Today many technical teams are not entirely satisfied with the current decentralized and cold architecture, that's why it demanded that a decentralized, sustainable and automatically distributed financial system appears: DeFi 2.0.

Among its main advantages you can find:

- It breaks the cold transaction mode of DeFi 1.0., seeking to establish tight horizontal connections and strong vertical links.

- Maintain liquid mining pools active enough to participate.

- Ecological governance and community decision-making rights. Members decide, not just based on enthusiasm and interest in participating in community activities.

- Providing only decentralized financial services. Here are born many decentralized financial innovations that will attract global geeks to complete technological innovation ideas and explode more high-quality financial projects. Innovations in any field are going to have unlimited imagination.

Decentralized financial DeFi 2.0 is the required stage out of the 1.0 era, although the two are going to coexist in technologies, but it certainly opens up a palette of options for new investments. It's gradually going to eliminate the cold, one-off mining incentives and continue to provide a more progressive driving force and it's going to be a world of financial ecology in the future.

Are there risks involved in investing in DeFi?

Yes, it does. It is an ecosystem that has great potential, and it also has its risks:

- There can be exorbitant movements in the price volatility of each asset.

- Hacks could happen.

- The ecosystem if you don't use it correctly can lead you to make mistakes that make you lose money.

- You can lose your wallet keys if you don't use a virtual wallet like Coinbase, Binace or Bit2Me which we explain below.

- An error in your cryptocurrency shipping address could cause you to lose your cryptocurrency.

Despite all that has been said, decentralized finance, like any interesting investment with great potential, has its risk and also its profit margin: the highest in the history of finance.

If you want to start investing you should take into account these general tips when making this type of investment:

- Don't invest more than you can lose.

- Diversify, don't just stick with one token or project, experiment and use different tools.
- Store and take good care of the access keys to these decentralized tools.
- Learn, be curious, make decisions based on your own analysis of projects, technology, don't let others decide for you.

The possibilities that DeFi has are many, it is a universe in itself within the blockchain world. The potential it has is incredible and there are many changes that we will see along the way.

That's why I recommend that before you start investing, you should objectively understand the growth potential and also the risks, so you can make better decisions and even develop them.

# 6. Decentralized Savings and Staking

When interest rates in the traditional world are close to zero, as they are as of the writing of this book, it's hard to generate any interest on traditional assets. If you've tried to open up a savings account to find that your interest rate is only 1 percent, or likely even less than that, how do you earn passive income? DeFi to the rescue, because there are ways that you can earn interest in one form or another on the blockchain.

There are two ways to earn interest with DeFi: one is to lend out your assets. The second way is by staking, which can potentially bring in more than with lending but of course you can also lose a lot of money by doing so. With blockchains that use Proof-of-Stake instead of Proof-of-Work, those who participate in validating the transactions earn rewards in that particular coin.

Proof-of-Work (PoW)

This is the original consensus algorithm that Bitcoin created. It's used to prove transactions and add new blocks to the chain. As you might recall from earlier, miners compete with each other to validate and get rewarded for their work.

There are two main advantages for this kind of consensus algorithm:

1. Difficult to attack: The math puzzles that must be solved to add a block to the chain are hard enough that attackers need a huge amount of computing power and a lot of time. It's not impossible, but it's certainly more difficult than, say, hacking into a computer network at the one point where everything links together.
2. "Rich" miners are not in charge: It doesn't matter how much coin you have, when mining what matters is your computations.

There are a couple of disadvantages as well:

**1. It's costly in different ways: As the chains grow longer, mining new blocks requires more and more raw computational power, not to mention actual electric power. Special software is needed to solve the problems as well. Now that mining is becoming increasingly more expensive, it's also becoming more concentrated and centralized.**

**The software and the computations are useless for anything else. They can't be adapted for college math classes, or science data gathering. In other words, all of that power is used in only one way, which is probably not sustainable for the planet.**

**2. In theory, a 51 percent attack could close down the chain: When a user or user group takes over the majority of the mining operations (51 percent), they can mine all the blocks and take all the rewards by shutting out all the other miners. They can reverse transactions and create forks in the chain. Once that happens, the chain is compromised, and other users leave.**

Proof-of-Stake (PoS)

An alternate algorithm, PoS was developed to address the issues of PoW. Miners can mine only the percentage of the coin they hold. For example, if a miner owns 5 percent of the available coins, then they're limited to mining 5 percent as well.

With this method, used on Ethereum and other networks, a miner would have to accumulate 51 percent of the currency, not 51 percent of the computing power. Someone who holds 51 percent of the crypto is less likely to instigate an attack against the crypto, because they would lose money as a result.

Validators for a block are randomly selected, depending on the amount they have staked.

Delegated Proof-of-Stake (DPoS)

Here's a democratic alternative to PoS invented by Daniel Larimer, a blockchain engineer who recognized that mining was too labor-intensive and too slow. He wanted a system that would be capable of 100,000 transactions per second, and PoW is too slow to accomplish that kind of speed (Crypto Stella, 2017).1

In DPoS, a fixed number of elected block producers (witnesses) add blocks to the chain in a round-robin type of selection order. Users vote for the witnesses, with their votes proportional to their stake, in a similar concept to PoS. Users can also choose to delegate their votes to another voter, who votes for them in the election.

Only the top witnesses are paid. There are plenty of backup witnesses since so many users are willing to take the duty. Though witnesses have a number of obligations, there's fierce competition to be one. Different platforms have varying numbers of elected witnesses; for example, Bitshare and Lisk have 101, while EOS and Steemit allow 21 witnesses.

All the competition puts some pressure on block producers to perform and make sure they're adding value. If a witness starts acting up or not adding enough value to the network, users stop voting for them, which removes them as witness. Since voting is ongoing, witnesses have constant incentive to take their duties seriously.

In addition to having elected witnesses and delegates, there are a couple of other differentiators compared to PoS. Block producers (witnesses) are the ones who create and sign new blocks. The block validators can be any user running a full node on the network. As a reminder, the block creators in PoS are referred to as validators, so the definition is different between the two.

A block is considered finalized and can't be reversed when it's finalized by 1 and ⅔ of the producers. If that doesn't happen, the next finalization is the "longest chain" rule. The longest chain is the one that most of the nodes accept as validated, and is generally the one with the most work on it. (More blocks and more work makes it more difficult for hackers to attack.)

Because the number of witnesses is limited, DPoS can handle many more transactions and is more scalable than PoW and even PoS. The price of this additional speed, however, is the centralization of the platform. Cartels could crop up, where users agree to vote for particular witnesses with the expectation that they'll be rewarded by the block producer in some way, or other means of bribing voters.

While it's an excellent solution for apps that require high throughput, centralization means it's not as secure as one that's decentralized. DPoS platforms, therefore, aren't usable as a base network like Ethereum, where platforms are built on top of its blockchain. They make sense for high-speed apps as a second layer on top of a secure platform. EOS is probably the best-known DPoS network. Others include BitShares, Steem, Ark, and Lisk.

Staking

On a blockchain that operates with PoS, you stake your coins, which allows you to participate in validating transactions (as miners do in PoW networks). Either you lock them into your wallet, or subscribe to an exchange that allows staking. You then earn a set percentage of your stake as a reward.

This is a larger market than you might expect. As staking is older than DeFi itself, in 2020 there was ten times more crypto staked than the value locked in decentralized finance (Liu, 2020).2 Although the rewards look much better than what can be earned through lending, they vary widely between different currencies.

Staking provides a higher yield than lending crypto for the same reason that high yield (junk) bonds do compared to regular corporate bonds: it's riskier. There are three main reasons why staking carries such high returns:

Coin price volatility

Except for stablecoins, as discussed earlier, most crypto fluctuates in price with their prices able to land anywhere in a huge range. Just like in the stock market or the housing market, the idea in the cryptocurrency market is to buy low and sell high.

Your staking reward could be paid to you at a time when the coin's price is high, and you'll be disappointed when it drops.

Payment in coin

If you've ever studied the stock market, you've probably heard people tell you not to put all your eggs in one basket. If all your savings is in one stock and the company goes out of business or into bankruptcy, you've just lost all your money.

If, on the other hand, you have a portfolio of 100 stocks (maybe through owning a mutual fund) and a company goes out of business, you may have lost some money, but not all of it. In theory you might not lose any money at all, depending on the weighting of the stocks in the portfolio and how well the others performed.

The rewards for staking a coin are paid in that coin, so you're adding eggs to your one basket. If the price seems to be on a downward spiral with no hope of recovering, you're probably not going to be overjoyed with having another of the same coin.

### Coin inflation

As new coins are minted, the supply is diluted, which causes inflation. Just as inflation lowers your stock or housing market returns, it reduces your currency value as well.

If you want a more consistent return for your stakes, you'll need to look for crypto with less price fluctuation and larger market cap. Do these characteristics ring a bell? They might if you've made stock investments, because in the stock market those are typically the S&P 500 stocks.

You probably think that your less risky crypto will return a lower level of rewards and you're absolutely right. In the same way that small cap stocks, which tend to be more volatile, also often earn higher returns than S&P 500 stocks, your lower-risk crypto will return less than more volatile currencies as well.

### Cold staking and staking pools

You can stake a coin by yourself, using just what's in your own online wallet, on a PoS blockchain. The downside is that in order to earn the most from your stake, you have to stay connected to the network 24/7. Has your power ever gone out in the summer, winter, during a severe storm, because squirrels chewed the wires from the connection box (true story), or beavers chewed through fiber optic cables to make their dam (also a true story)? Even a brief power outage severs your connection to the network and sends you back to square one. You may be limited in your stake's earning potential if you choose to do it this way.

Another method is known as **cold staking.** Rather than storing your coin in an online wallet that must be accessible 24/7, you can store it offline in a hardware wallet. The coins must stay in that offline wallet because if you move them to a different address, you'll lose the ability to earn rewards.

Or you could join a **stakepool**. This way, you're not running the connection on your own hardware or on a virtual private network (VPN). Stakepool operators have the hardware to stay connected, generally with a master node on the blockchain that is reserved for the network only.

By joining a staking pool, not only do you not have to be concerned about local outages, but the pool's larger stake size means it's more likely to write a block or vote on it to be added to the blockchain. That gives you more of a chance to earn rewards.

### Staking Requirements

How much you can make by staking varies with a number of factors, including the size of the pool, the amount of coin that's locked, and the block's rewards. The longer you **hodl** (hold on for dear life, or stake), the higher your payout will usually be, depending, of course, on the value of the coin itself. The staking rules vary according to the blockchain and the coin, so you'll want to investigate them before you decide to stake.

You might also have to run a certain operating system or other technical requirements, because you are contributing to the security of the blockchain so there usually are some minimums in terms of speed and so forth.

For the staking itself, the coin will usually specify how many you need as a minimum as well. Not every network allows cold staking in an offline wallet; your alternatives would be either staying tethered to the network 24/7/365 or joining a staking pool (if available).

You'll need an online wallet (unless you're cold staking) that supports staking. The coins you buy will normally need to season for a couple of days in your wallet before they're available for you to stake.

ETH is one of the most popular staking coins as of this writing, since staking only became possible on the chain with the December 2020 release of the first phase of the Ethereum 2.0 launch. This phase created the Beacon chain, which is the PoS chain (the first version of Ethereum is PoW). Other coins include ZCoin, Tezos, and ICON among others.

# 7. Tips For Investment In Defi

As it is evident from the name, DeFi that it is a term that refers to decentralized finance. It is a network that is based on blockchain and consists of tools used by digital financial that comprise all digital securities and cryptocurrency to NFTs (Non-Fungible Tokens) and CBDCs (Central Bank Digital Currency). DeFi is a peer-to-peer financial service that licenses you to trade crypto and other relevant services. DeFi is dependent upon the Ethereum blockchain and cryptocurrencies. The DeFi market grew bigger in the year 2020. Statistics recorded raised from $700 million to $13 billion. Presently, this figure has gone up to $40 billion.

The global financial systems are evolving and transforming digitally. This displays that the DeFi financial system has a lot of potentials and can become even stronger and draw the attention of the world. But it is important that you know and understand the asset first and then how to invest in the market.

DeFi Assets

Trading DeFi assets, which are tokens representing DeFi networks, applications, or protocols, is one of the ways to invest in DeFi, this usually involves buying low and selling high. Not everyone can do this because there is a high risk involved and is extremely volatile. Nonetheless, the prospects thrive. A few examples are Uniswap (UNI), Terra (LUNA), Wrapped Bitcoin (WBTC), and Chainlink (LINK).

DeFi Staking

Another option for achieving passive income based on DeFi is staking. In staking funds are locked by users in a crypto wallet and they participate in maintaining the operations of a PoS blockchain system, which results in users getting a rate of interest that is already defined. When everyone is offering negative rates of interest, receiving a reasonable interest rate on your holdings, especially if you intend on selling them anyways is worthwhile. Assets worth a total of around $21 to $23 billion are staked on DeFi platforms, as of January 2021.

DeFi Yield Farming

Yield farming has become viral and is based on Ethereum. DeFi is an all-inclusive category of the peer-to-peer service, self-custody, KYC-less, finance apps that are based on Ethereum, but yield farming labels popular enticements program where liquidity is provided in return for a DeFi application.

## DeFi Lending & Lending Protocol

Users are allowed to give away their crypto to someone else and in return earn interest on the loan on DeFi Lending platforms. Defi lending benefits lenders as well as borrowers. Not only does it offer options for margin trading, but it also enables long-term investors to lend assets and earn higher interest rates. Moreover, it also allows users to access fiat currency credit to borrow loans at lower rates than DEX. Furthermore, it can be sold by the users on a centralized exchange for a cryptocurrency and then lend to a DEX.

## DeFi Funds

Trusts and Funds are another way to invest in the DeFi network. This is the most welcoming way for beginners to get acquainted with DeFi. Bitwise's DeFi Index Fund, Grayscale's Diversified DeFi fund, and Galaxy Digital's DeFi index tracker fund are some examples of DeFi funds.

## Risk vs. Reward with DeFi

What makes DeFi an eye-catching and possibly profitable investment is the multiplicity of investment prospects, as well as the sustained progression of the market. However, just like with any investment, this also has risks that market investors should be made familiar with before they dive in. Not only is there a risk of the impact the crypto volatility may have but there are also security and scam risks with DeFi, that can be attributed to the DeFi protocols relying on smart contracts having weak spots that can be exploited.

The weaknesses can be decreased by the DeFi market, the technology running it, as well as the required regulations that will unavoidably be achieved, and the appeal of this digital finance system will increase. So all one has to do is be patient, be smart, and never miss a good opportunity.

Decentralized Finance (DeFi) has gathered a lot of courtesy recently. The innovation has been led by Uniswap and Compound.

Some distinguished developments include:

- DeFi market capitalization has surpassed $10 Bn
- Uniswap has outdone Coinbase

Yearn Finance has gone beyond the worth of Bitcoin for a solitary unit, it's all-time high touching the $43,000 mark.

Nonetheless, the DeFi landscape has a dark spot that is deeply hidden. The market has been tainted by rug pulls and hacks. Some people went through huge losses of money. It is significant to know the risk areas and stay safe.

Some tips to help you to take better Yield Farming decisions are given below:

1. High APY does not always guarantee high returns:

The very first thing that deceives people is high APY. For numerous projects, the opening APY is more than 10,000%. It is a great way to upsurge your money. Two questions arise:

The first one is will the High Yield be maintainable? Assess the timeline of the high yield. The supply in the early days is devaluated which results in high yields. It is halved in rapid progressions. However, this falls significantly over a short period.

The second question is will you be able to sell at a profit? Most of the time if you are able to earn a considerable amount in the early days of devaluation, you will be unable to sell the token as a majority of them will be locked. Assess the number of earned tokens you'd be able to sell.

For instance, three-quarters of Token in Luaswap is locked for initial 16 months.

2. Invest in Those Tokens That Have Authentic Use Cases:

Question yourself about why do you need the token given by the project. For many projects governance is highly overvalued. Can the token be used in any other way apart from Governance?

Are you aware of the fact that UNI can be used as collateral to get loans on other platforms? That is an actual convenience that gives UNI worth. Many other DeFi tokens are acquisitive and greedy without proper usefulness and are intended to fall.

3. Only invest in Audited Projects:

Invest in a project only and only if it is audited by a renowned organization. It is mandatory for the code of the project to be audited.

Many people invested in the yet "in production" project Eminence, when Andre Cronje revealed his connection with it due to his good reputation. But since the project was still not completed and was not audited, it was unavoidably hacked and the hacker stole $15M.

4. Inclusion of Gas Fees in your profit calculations:

It should be noted that in the present days of high gas fees the actual investment consists of the fees for buying Pair of tokens in Uniswap, accepting Liquidity Pool Pair in Uniswap, approving LP Staking in the Yield Farming Protocol, Actual Staking in Yield Farming Protocol, Unstake in Yield Farming Protocol, sell yield token in Uniswap, Removing Liquidity in Uniswap.

All these things add up to be the total fee that cannot be neglected and should always be a part of the profit calculations.

5. When Do You Plan to Enter Yield Farming project?

The time you enter a project is also very crucial because after the first few days the market inclines to fall. So it should be carefully decided when you want to enter the project. If you plan to enter a project after some time, which can be as early as a day. You cannot say that there is a selling pressure created which is from the first day's profit.

6. Take Impermanent Loss into consideration:

The amount of tokens that you have combined in the liquidity pools is adjusted by Uniswap as the worth of yield farming tokens falls. What will happen is that the amount of your yield farming token will raise and your second token (for instance ETH) will fall.

This will fall in the ratio of your unique pool submission. Your whole worth will be lower than what you would have got if you would have just held these two tokens. However, it should be noted that temporary loss is not sustained till the time the liquidity is removed. This problem can be solved by a long-time liquidity supply in the pool.

7. Don't Forget to Calculate the Price on Over-all Supply:

In the beginning, the token price is pretty high due to the low circulation but as more and more tokens are in circulation in the upcoming days. the price of the token will fall. Ascertain the position where you want your invested project to land in the CoinMarketCap ranking and try to conclude its unit price on the basis of another project with a similar supply in that CMC ranking. You will be surprised to find how low the unit price could reach!

There are high risks involved when investing in DeFi. You should only invest the amount if you are prepared for losses. Invest only in trustworthy projects. Do not invest only because of the fear of missing out. Spend some money on the cost of learning.

# 8. What Is Defi Marketplace

The terms 'cryptocurrency', 'blockchain', and 'Bitcoin' have revolutionized the world entirely. Since the time when these terms were introduced tons of modernization has been witnessed in this space. DeFi is one such trend that has taken over the world of crypto over the past year, especially after BTC reached a new all-time high. Just in a short amount of time these decentralized marketplaces have made great progress, and have resulted in a very substantial modification in the world of crypto. If you are uncertain as to which DeFi marketplace is best suited for you this piece will help you figure it all out.

DeFi marketplaces are decentralized marketplaces which means that there is no middleman involved. The fundamental idea of DeFi marketplaces is very comparable to blockchain, in which the software can be downloaded by a user who can get directly linked to everyone else using the software at that instant of time.

This is how an extraordinary level of transparency is guaranteed by the platform, around the rules and working of the marketplace. Another characteristic of blockchain, which is also followed by the DeFi marketplaces is its permanence, meaning that data cannot be deleted or withdrawn by any means once it is logged into the secured system of a blockchain.

What makes DeFi marketplaces important is that centralized exchanges like Binance and Coinbase would not be used for trading if the idea of decentralization brought into view by digital currencies was better received and loved by the audiences.

Top 5 Defi Marketplaces based on Transaction Volume:

Below is a list of the top 5 decentralized marketplaces based on total trading volume concerning data from the last 30 days.

**PancakeSwap**

PancakeSwap is a digital exchange that was developed for the exchange of BEP20 Binance Smart Chain tokens. PancakeSwap uses the Automated market maker (AMM) model and has a market value of somewhat $16 billion.

This is how trading could be done against a liquidity pool by the users of the platform. The platform permits users to credit an amount of money into the pool, getting LP or liquidity provider tokens, which are traded for the money. The other name for the Liquidity Provider (LP) tokens is FLIP tokens.

### UniSwap

UniSwap is another protocol for Ethereum's automated market maker, UniSwap also has a market value of $16 billion, just like PancakeSwap. It was launched in the year 2018, the platform is termed as a comparatively simple and smart border for swapping ERC20 tokens.

Analogous to PancakeSwap, a model has been formalized for the creation of a liquidity pool of reserves. The platform is used by liquidity providers and traders as one open-source frontend. UniSwap could be considered as a pioneer in this arena, in order to continue its leadership, it launched UniSwap v3 just recently.

### MDEX

The smartest exchange innovation of recent times, MDEX is an automatic market-making decentralized exchange that functions around the fundamentals of fund pools for its users. The market volume of MDEX is well over $15 billion and it operates around Ethereum and Heco Chain.

It runs as a single hybrid platform and is a combination of the low transaction fees from the Heco chain and the vast ecosystem of Ethereum.

### SushiSwap

An exchange platform based on the Ethereum blockchain network, SushiSwap is a rapidly developing DeFi marketplace. This platform has a market value of over $77 million, and it strives to encourage users to trade in crypto.

In order for it to achieve the trade goals, SushiSwap functions over the liquidity pool.

### BurgerSwap

BurgerSwap is known to be the very first democratized decentralized American Metal Market (AMM), it operates on the binance smart chain. The market volume of BurgerSwap is around $51 million. BurgerSwap is one of the most noticeable and trustworthy platforms and enables any user to create proposals that let them review the transaction fees, block rewards, and make complete use of other such exchange parameters.

DeFi and blockchain function in the same way in terms of not needing any traders and the storage of transaction data on different decentralized systems. DeFi currencies serve a multitude of motives, such as easy transactions which are comparable to the functions of a virtual currency like Bitcoin. Unlike currencies like bitcoin, Defi currencies can also be used for intricate financial operations. Not only this but using DeFi marketplaces enable you to stay true to the original vision of cryptocurrencies and blockchain tech.

# 9. Challenges and Risks of DeFi

Now you'll get a closer look at some of the risks that DeFi and its investors face currently.

These may change and evolve over time, depending on how the sector moves into the future. Some of the problems are likely to solve themselves if DeFi gets off the ground that it's currently on but others don't have obvious answers.

Perception is reality

For many people, decentralized finance doesn't mean anything. They may have heard of cryptocurrencies in general, and they've probably heard of Bitcoin. Both these terms, however, have a bad reputation with a lot of ordinary people who don't know much about finance or technology.

The reputational problems begin with the original whitepaper published in 2008 that posited an alternative finance solution that avoided financial institutions. The name on the whitepaper is Satoshi Nakamoto, but to this day, it's unclear whether this is an actual person or a group of people. Which is unfortunate because creating peer-to-peer alternatives is a logical reaction to many of the events leading up to the Great Recession.

At first, one of the major communities for Bitcoin was Silk Road, a marketplace on the dark web that allowed trade in anything, whether or not the item was legal. One of the biggest trading markets was for drugs, both legal and not. Silk Road was seized by the US government in 2013, and that made a big splash in the media. The message was not that Bitcoin presented an alternative to traditional finance, but that crypto enabled bad guys to do things that were illegal.

A religious friend of mine told me that she would never use cryptocurrency because it was used for human sex trafficking. That may be true or not, and certainly plenty of traffickers use fiat currency anyway; she's not alone in believing that's what crypto is used for.

The Mt. Gox scandal didn't help either. The whole premise of bitcoin, the blockchain, and distributed ledgers is security, that no one can tinker with the blocks. Magic: The Gathering Online eXchange, founded in 2010, began using Bitcoin as a currency.

In 2014, it was forced to file for bankruptcy. Users complained that they couldn't withdraw their coins, which turned out to be due to an attacker that had been draining accounts for years. This was not supposed to happen in the secure cryptocurrency world. Other thefts, such as the 2021 grab that occurred in Turkey, are also on the general public's radar.

Finally, even those who aren't attuned to the world of blockchain or crypto have seen the headlines when Bitcoin rose spectacularly in price, and also when it dropped just as spectacularly. Investors lost a lot of their risk tolerance in and around the Great Recession, so having something called currency that is wildly unstable doesn't give them a lot of confidence. (Yes, stablecoins exist, but they're not as well-known as Bitcoin.)

In order to be taken seriously and to become a true mechanism for an alternate financial system, more people have to adopt the blockchain for themselves and their businesses. Which means that DeFi has to shed crypto's bad reputation.

That may mean doing things differently in order to capture the public's trust. The NYSE hasn't endured any theft scandals lately; neither have other stock and futures exchanges. Although crypto was also intended to avoid central banks, the Federal Reserve, Bank of England, the European Central Bank and other major central banks across the globe have not suffered anything along the lines of Mt. Gox or Silk Road either.

While crypto currently is good for speculation, average people need to trust and feel relatively safe with the system they use for their money. Right now, the blockchain is not providing them with the sense of security they need.

Relative youth

Some of the issues with DeFi are due to the relative infancy of the idea. It was only conceived this century, and we're not very far into the 21st yet. Difficulties such as high price volatility are at least partly a result of the markets still being relatively small. As more people begin to adopt the system, some of that will subside.

It's a bit of a chicken-or-egg dilemma. People don't trust crypto because it fluctuates so much, but it fluctuates so much because not enough people are in the crypto market. These types of growing pains are typical for a lot of technology, especially this century.

It also means that the theory behind the blockchain is only now being practically tested, with the expected results that the original designers didn't consider. Although, in theory, the Mt. Gox theft should have been impossible, it wasn't.

Crypto designers didn't spend enough time considering the security of all the entities that touched Bitcoin. They assumed that the block security protocols and difficulty mining blocks would solve all the problems. They were wrong.

When it comes to money, most of the public wants to know it's safe when they put it somewhere. Having a lot of people lose a lot of value because the designers didn't consider security everywhere they needed to is not exactly a recipe for trust.

New tech always has bugs. People are likely to forgive growing pains when those pains happen to a piece of software, not when bugs affect the money that they need to live on. Major financial institutions, central banks, and exchanges spend a lot of money defending against attacks and implementing new security protocols to keep a Mt. Gox from happening to them.

That's a lesson DeFi must learn if it expects to be widely adopted. What are the potential failure points, and how do you protect against them?

Cars and dot-coms in the 20th Century

DeFi is young, and youthful marketplaces and concepts often drive speculative bubbles. People get caught up in FOMO (fear of missing out) and start investing once they see prices being driven higher and higher. (Which are almost always countered by a traumatic thud when prices come back down to earth. Gravity is real.)

It also leads to a lot of innovators trying to get in on the craze, without necessarily understanding what they're doing. New technology in particular seems to convince both inventors and investors that the new marketplace is totally new and revolutionary, and that the old paradigms no longer apply. However, human nature doesn't change. More on that in the next section.

Earlier in the book you read about Warren Buffett and his comparison of the early car marketplace in the US to the dot-com boom. There were 100 car manufacturers in the early 20th Century, and towards the end there were four. If you'd invested in one car manufacturer early on, you basically had a 1-in-25 chance of picking a winner. How would you have beaten those odds? Maybe you would have gotten lucky.

When dot-coms came around, the investors who were interested were older (typically Baby Boomers) and didn't really understand the internet. The inventors thought they knew everything, especially once the investors started throwing money at any web address that ended in dotcom. However, the laws of supply and demand don't change just because a new technology has entered the Thunderdome. And so the bubble ended in a predictable crash.

Even in the early 2000s, people set aside long-known investment truths to throw themselves into a frenzy. There is a lot of blame to go around for the Great Recession, everything from government policies to individual greed to corporate greed.

Once the floodgates opened, everyone could buy their own house that they couldn't afford in reality, thanks to forged documents and NINJA loans (no job, no income or assets) from questionable lenders and their suppliers.

The idea was that homeowners could buy a bigger house with a lower interest rate loan, paying the interest only, and then refinancing when the principal payments started. This presupposed that housing prices, which had recently begun to blow the roof, would keep going up. Which is not at all how finance works - no market continues to rise indefinitely - but people chose to ignore this inconvenient fact.

The banks got busy creating mortgage loan packages for their greedy investors - interest rates had fallen and investors were searching for yield. The banks didn't even know what they were doing, and very few, if any, of the officers responsible for creating these mortgage packages (known as CMOs and CDOs) understood the math.

The mortgage originators didn't care that their loans were unlikely to perform. They knew the banks would buy the worst mortgage and stuff it into a package and sell it to investors. That's decentralization (in a way) for you, and it ended very, very badly for the potential homeowners and all the people who lost jobs in the ensuing recession.

Currently, at least in crypto (as opposed to blockchain or DeFi), there are a bunch of people who don't know what they're doing and investors (and inventors) who have joined in the latest frenzy. After all, we are in a low interest rate environment, and holding coins can bring you more yield than what you'll find at a bank or in a bond. As the saying goes (usually attributed to Mark Twain), "History never repeats itself but it often rhymes."[1]

You'll note that cars continue to be driven, some dotcoms have become enormous enterprises that employ thousands of people, and people continue to take out mortgages. The question is whether DeFi is pre- or post-bubble. If it's pre-bubble, then it makes sense for investors and average people to wait until the market shakes out and separates the companies with a good chance of succeeding from those that don't.

Human nature and centralization

It may come as a surprise to many libertarians, but many of the rules and regulations around traditional finance were designed to prevent abuses and issues experienced in the past. They're not (usually) made up just to frustrate people.

Some people rail about the Federal Reserve and its power. It was chartered in the early 20th Century and originally designed to maintain full employment (which is not the same as 100 percent employment, by the way.) It only received inflation-fighting power after the oil crisis led to stagflation in the 1970s.

Licensing requirements for stockbrokers and insurance sellers are there to ensure that the people selling financial products have at least a tiny bit of familiarity with how the markets work and what's legal and what's not. That's because in the 1920s there were too many snake-oil salesmen selling phony stock certificates and other fraud schemes to credulous investors.

Selling snake oil with no compunction, making a buck off a credulous mark, and ignoring the consequences of your actions are fundamental to capitalism, especially in the United States. When the consequences are dangerous and/or life-threatening, however, the government arguably has a responsibility to address them.

For example, California's tighter emissions standards aren't because Californians hate cars. Los Angeles is completely surrounded and bisected by huge freeways, because it became a major city after cars became popular. LA's geography means smog from vehicle exhaust gets trapped over the city and its environs, especially on hot days. The state tightened emissions standards so Californians could breathe. Los Angeles County is one of the largest in the country in terms of population, so without the standards a lot of people would have needlessly died.

Note, however, that the tighter standards are due to government intervention. Conventional libertarian wisdom holds that the free market solves all problems, but that's prima facie wrong. The car manufacturers didn't voluntarily decide to make engines cleaner so people could breathe.

The tobacco industry knew that their product was poisonous and led to early death for decades, but they tried to squash the release of that information. The invisible hand of the market allowed them to continue to sicken and kill people, until the documents came to light. Even so, the government had to intervene by restricting tobacco advertising to children and taking other measures.

In other words, the 20th and 21st Centuries have shown that there are bad actors out there and that the free market doesn't always solve the problem, even though it should in theory. People want to have a place where they can go to complain or get their problems straightened out. Automated bots don't do it; people want to actually talk to someone to get their problem solved, especially when it comes to money.

Centralized exchanges and platforms have this capability. On the other hand, that goes against the ethos of decentralization in the first place! While centralization would no doubt appeal to many ordinary people who are concerned about not having anyone to turn to when something goes wrong, other users will want to ensure that the blockchain remains decentralized. If it doesn't catch on with the public, many of the current problems (such as lack of liquidity) will remain.

Competitive landscape: traditional system

You've seen how much a decentralized system with fewer intermediaries can potentially benefit people across the globe by giving them more access to capital without needing a sizable chunk of money to begin with.

The existing traditional players have a lot of power and they're closely linked with government structures as well. Any alternative that's going to be widely adopted has to be recognized as being just as secure as the existing structure, and DeFi currently is not.

You might think (or hope) that the failure of governments and banking institutions during the Great Recession might have an effect on people who use the current system. After all, only one (foreign) banker in the US went to jail, and none of the others did. In fact, some of the banks that played a big part in the meltdown are stronger than ever.

Depending on your political beliefs, there are easy scapegoats on the "other" side: conservatives blame greedy homeowners and the government for loosening lending standards. Liberals blame the mortgage companies who made bad loans and the banks who packaged the loans. The underlying structure, however, has largely escaped comment, at least among the general public and the media. Most people are not blaming the centralized system for being the culprit.

Not to mention that the existing system already has a lot of political power, in addition to money. Its members regularly lobby the government, and because of their deep pockets, they're the ones to listen to.

Can you buy, for example, Facebook's Libra coin? Recall that it was pulled due to concerns that it would affect the traditional system. If you're considering a cryptocurrency that's usable around the world it's not a bad idea to base it on a basket of currencies, not just the US dollar or euro or yuan.

That's not a terrible business model. Although you can certainly argue that an entity other than a social media company known for privacy invasion should launch it. It was pulled, not because it wouldn't succeed, but because it might succeed too well.

The blockchain will need to figure out a way to work around the power structure coziness to attract more business.

Competitive landscape: apps

There already is an arena that cuts down on intermediaries and costs, and uses automation to simplify financial transactions. It's known as **fintech**, which is the universe of financial apps that are available to many users around the globe.

There are apps to help people looking for insurance policies to compare and contrast policies from a variety of companies. You can get a term life insurance quote in seconds. You can deposit checks by taking pictures of them on your phone instead of hitting the teller or even the ATM. You can pay bills automatically from your checking account, or even your rewards credit card.

If you're a business owner, there are already automated payroll systems and HR departments. You can hire a CFO, COO, accountant, etc., on a consulting basis and pull up their bios immediately to see if you want to hire them.

From a user perspective, these companies are already regulated in most countries. There's no need to change to a widely fluctuating currency to take advantage of automation and machine learning to get a loan, for example. That means if something goes wrong you have a number to call, which the average person really wants in a service provider.

Human error (developers)

Tech works really well - when it's working! We've all been at a store when their connection goes down or their automated sales system stops working or had some issue with software, etc. Almost every software release goes out with bugs, because the prevailing culture is to just ship it and let the users tell you about the bugs. Again, people are often willing to deal with it when it comes to software but not necessarily when that software is dealing with their money.

There's no guarantee that a developer creating smart contracts can make sure they're bug-free. Things often get missed, even when you're working with open-source code or programs designed to be easily read, like Go programming language. Of course, there's no manager to call if the auto-execute feature doesn't work like it was supposed to.

For example, suppose that an investor buys an option contract on blockchain which is designed to automatically run if the option's in the money at expiration. A bug prevents the program from executing. The user on the other side of the trade might not mind, but that investor will. Who do they go to?

It's not the other side's fault that the 3rd party smart contract didn't work, so they're not going to make the investor whole. Who will? The developer? Will the investor even know who the developer is? Some platforms offer insurance, but what if the users decide they don't want to pay out that claim? That's the kind of uncertainty that investors are not willing to risk money on.

Human error (users)

In theory, pushing authority down the chain is the most democratic thing to do, and it (theoretically) makes sense for the end user to have more control over their financial tech. That's not always how it works best in practice, though!

Consider California's ballot initiatives. They were conceived as a way for the voter to register their personal preferences on issues that achieve a certain amount of signatures, rather than having the elected representatives make those decisions. Great idea, in theory.

Most people in the 21st Century are awash in information overload. The 2020 election included 26 ballot initiatives, many of them confusingly named. In some cases, if you supported Cause X, you would actually have to vote against the ballot measure named Save Cause X.

Even if you read the voter information guide, it's a lot to wade through. Many people don't have or want to take the time to wade through it, and so they rely on sound bites or what their friends told them about it.

In a similar vein, there are still people (and not all of them over 65) who look frantically for the "any" key when they're on a tech support call. Giving them more authority over their tech choices might not actually help them make better decisions, as much as we'd like to think it would.

Poor user experiences

Most blockchain users currently are at least reasonably tech-savvy, and can figure out what they need to know or do when presented with an interface that isn't intuitive. Though they may still be annoyed when things are taking too long to wind their way onto a block, or the system is otherwise slow in processing something.

In order for more people to adopt the technology, it has to be friendlier to people who aren't tech savvy. You've probably heard the howls of outrage every time a social media platform changes the format of something its users like. Even if the GUI is simpler, it still takes time for the public to get used to it and get comfortable with it.

People won't use something that's too hard to navigate. If they have to wrap their heads not only around the idea of blockchain itself, and then figure out how to use a particular platform, they're going to give up and go back to the app or their bank where they know how to get things done. Blockchain developers need to take the next step of not just focusing on how to solve a particular problem, but to make it easy for people to get the answer.

Poor performance

Blockchain processing can take longer than similar processes in the traditional system, due to the large number of nodes that are involved. Centralized systems don't rely on tens or hundreds of computers scattered around the globe, and their transaction times are therefore usually much faster.

While some networks boast of their performance speeds of so many transactions (tx) per second, that's usually in a controlled environment with a much more limited number of nodes than what real-world users experience.

### Higher transaction costs

Clients (or users) of DeFi do a lot of the computational work through decentralized systems. While the blockchain platforms are faster and lighter, it may take a user's computer some time to actually perform the calculations and get the digital signatures necessary for game or wallet transactions.

The more layers of cryptography (that secure the transactions), the longer it takes. From the user's perspective, it slows them down.

### P2P networking

In essence, information on one transaction is sent twice: once from the user to the block producer, which may distribute it out to a group of peers. Then back to the user once confirmed, which may use a completely different set of peers to validate.

Because the paths are randomly distributed, they can't be optimized for performance the way transactions in the traditional system can. Their networks are designed and built for speed. While a decentralized system is safer from malicious participants and central points of failure, it can't guarantee any kind of data transfer performance.

This part of the process can also be very time-consuming on the blockchain, which many users will understand as bad performance from the system.

### Consensus algorithm

Whether PoS or PoW algorithms are used, mining and voting take time. If the platform or network is having some kind of tech issue, there will be more delays.

The more participants on a blockchain, the slower it will be. The ability to scale up is something developers are currently working on. Ethereum's use of shards may help to solve this part of the problem and speed up the transfers, resulting in a better experience for the users.

## Liquidity issues

As noted earlier, this is somewhat of a chicken-or-egg conundrum. Crypto markets tend to be illiquid because there aren't as many participants but of course people don't want to participate in a market with no liquidity!

Why is liquidity so important? It may not be an issue for early adopters, investors who already have plenty of liquid assets elsewhere, or speculators who don't mind taking on enormous amounts of risk. Many people (especially in the US) live paycheck to paycheck, and one of their biggest problems is the lack of cash in case of emergencies (Roberts, 2020).2

The general public wants to be able to access their money when they need it. If they lose their jobs, or the house needs an unexpected repair, or whatever the issue might be, they don't want their funds sitting in a market where they can't get to them. Or a market where one day their holdings are worth $5,000 and the next $500.

Paper (or digital) wealth is great to look at. If you can't transform your millions in crypto into a reasonable equivalent in fiat currency, crypto isn't actually worth very much. While stablecoins may be more liquid, you can't earn very much with them, at least compared to other kinds of coins.

Investors ask for higher rates of return for illiquid investments; after all, they're riskier. The cryptocurrency world needs some mechanism to reliably deliver the higher rates if the markets stay small, in order to compensate the investors for taking on an illiquid investment.

Sustainability

The fact is that the earth is getting warmer due to human activity. The Greenhouse Effect is due to the Earth's atmosphere trapping heat that would otherwise dissipate out into space. Certain gases that have increased due to human activity contribute to the effect, including methane, nitrous oxide (NO), and carbon dioxide (CO2). Burning fossil fuels results in much more NO and CO2, which makes the planet heat up faster. While three degrees warmer doesn't seem like it could do much damage, it would cause glaciers to melt and a number of coastal cities would disappear underwater, such as Osaka, Shanghai, Rio de Janeiro, and Miami (Holder et al, 2017).3 Land that is now used to grow food will no longer support agriculture because the temperatures will be too hot. And so on.

Blockchains that use mining and PoW algorithms use a lot of power, much of which is generated by burning fossil fuels like oil and coal. That's not a sustainable practice, not to mention that many people who are concerned about the environment will refuse to use it. (Remember the artists who pulled back NFTs due to climate concerns.)

Fortunately, one solution is PoS consensus that doesn't require massive amounts of power to build and validate blocks. The general public will need to be educated about the difference, because if all they know is Bitcoin and mining, they'll be worried about blockchain's effect on the Earth.

Blockchain can actually be a force for good when it comes to the environment. Using it for the supply chain means less waste, and traceability means less fraud and fewer natural resources devoted to fraudulent transactions and products.

The networks, however, have to be PoS and not PoW. What happens to Bitcoin? It's not sustainable. The network has constrained the system to mine only 21 billion coins in total, and as of this writing slightly less than 19 million have been mined.

Due to the way Bitcoins are structured, it's not expected that the last one will be mined until 2140 (Phillips et al, 2021). By then, unless things change significantly, the earth will be experiencing serious issues with warming as discussed above.

As long as DeFi remains on PoS networks, they won't be contributing to global warming. If Bitcoin doesn't change the way it runs, that might not matter. When catastrophe arrives, it doesn't really matter how we got there.

## Practical Tools in Decentralized Finance Risk

- Use data in Ethereum blockchain with Etherscan.

Etherscan, an Ethereum Blockchain network Explorer website, is a handy tool for examining transactions and the condition of the Ethereum Blockchain network. It may be used to look up and verify any trade or transaction on the blockchain network. The majority of blockchain networks have their explorer.

It is advised that you use Etherscan to monitor the wallet transactions and input your Ethereum wallet address. Examine the recipient addresses of any recent transactions you've done, and if there are any odd situations, like any bizarre behavior, address them as soon as feasible.

- Use Coingecko to get the most recent information on cryptocurrencies as well as the most recent price changes

This is a very handy tool for getting full and reference information on different currencies, as well as price fluctuations and market capacity. You may also utilize Coingecko to get the most up-to-date information on liquidity and Farming Pools, as well as the current APY, the number of audits linked with that platform, and the total value locked.

You can get the most detailed information about liquidity pools in various blockchain networks by utilizing the LiquidityFolio platform. You may also verify your presence in multiple pools by inputting the wallet address into this platform.

- The Zapper platform aims to make fund management easier in decentralized finance.

A Defi fund management program aims to deliver services on decentralized finance platforms so that all assets may be viewed in the dashboard. Furthermore, the platform aims to simplify it by offering the most significant liquidity, Farm pools, and relevant filters.

- Use the Zerion platform to conduct all key activities in Defi via a good user interface.

It is a useful tool for controlling all critical processes in the Defi ecosystem. Using this platform, you may track your portfolio in a chart format that is very useful and thorough in presenting portfolio assets. It even keeps track of NFT assets. The fact that this platform has a nice user interface is one of its most significant features.

There are additional parts for Exchange, Borrow, and a search bar for key liquidity pools and YF sites on the network. Another benefit of these platforms is their partnerships with DEXs and the simplicity they may conduct transactions.

For instance, during the initial 1inch Airdrop, the 1Inch platform that distributed 600 tokens to its participants had some initial delays owing to increased traffic from participants claiming coins and requesting transfers to their wallets. Participants that checked the 1Inch Twitter account and learned about the system's connection with Zerion, on the other hand, were able to move Airdrop coins to their Zerion wallet quickly.

- The YF Tools platform offers significant Defi-related tools and resources.

This tool includes features like estimating the Impermanent Loss, the size of Collateral, and more. One of the benefits of this platform is that it allows you to learn about the most significant and current issues in decentralized finance, which can be found in the Resource section.

You may use the Impermanent Loss estimator equally and obtain the most recent Ethereum gas Fees under the Tools section. This platform includes a liquidity pool search bar. However, it differs in that it has extremely great and unique filters. Filters like APY rates, smart contract risk, and Impermanent Loss, as well as numerous platforms which provide decentralized finance, collateral type, and coins in Pools, and benefits for participation in different Pools, are all extremely helpful.

- Trade through the @GaspriceTrackerBot bot on Telegram, and set notification for the right time.

This bot is designed to give recent information about Ethereum Blockchain network transaction costs. This bot can also send out notifications when fees are low or warnings when the gas fee charges are high.

- Use the Gasnow site to get the optimal gas fee for you based on the time priority that is most convenient for you before conducting any transactions on the Ethereum blockchain network.

This site, which is backed by Sparkpool, one of the largest Ethereum network mining pools, provides the most exact amount of gas fees in four distinct periods. Another benefit of this site is that it provides a helpful chart of the amount of gas fee vs the number of completed transactions that can forecast the traffic on the Ethereum blockchain.

- Determine the risk profile of smart contracts and helper tools by visiting Defiyield.info

It is with no question among the most crucial decentralized finance management systems. This tool may look for liquidity pools and Vaults from other platforms to invest in. One of the essential aspects of Defiyield is that it displays the audits that have been completed and the risk level of smart contracts in the decentralized finance landscape.

It equally contains the Impermanent Loss estimator, which has the most precise and user interface. Stopping Ethereum Network Transactions and a Gas Cost Monitor are two other significant features of this platform.

- Use lending management features with the Defisaver platform.

It's among the most crucial instruments in the loan and borrowing landscape. We could effectively safeguard our Collateral against loans acquired from various sites due to this technology, giving us peace of mind.

We may also return our loan by generally making just a single transaction, which saves us money on trading costs. Another helpful function of this platform is the ability to transform collaterals to one another or move your holdings from one network to another in a single transaction. In addition, when a participant launches Smart wallet on the platform, a Maker CDP is immediately generated for them.

You may equally apply the Loan Shifter function after developing a smart wallet. In brief, DefiSaver lowers trading costs in the lending and borrowing landscape while also making fund and collateral management super simple.

- Benefit from the new decentralized finance services in lending by using the Instadapp platform.

The platform has also shown to be highly beneficial in the lending industry and strategy execution. Instadapp is recognized for its unique approach to participant service in this domain.

The use of Uniswap LP coins in leverage and collateral strategies, for instance, is highly intriguing and creative in the most recent upgrade of its services. Professional decentralized finance participants have been able to boost their revenue via the fees of AMM platforms thanks to this innovative approach.

- Furucombo allows you to do several transactions in one.

The platform is intended for participants already acquainted with Defi and want to make complicated hybrid transactions easier. Furucombo allows you to perform a set of complicated decentralized finance protocols strategies in one transaction. You may equally gain ideas from other example combinations in the Explore area and utilize them to optimize your trades.

- You may browse and get rapid and classified access to decentralized applications by utilizing dappradar.

With the proliferation of decentralized apps on various blockchain networks, classified access and exploration using realistic filters are becoming increasingly important.

This platform serves as a conduit between blockchain network developers and participants. Statistical reporting, fund management, and recent information on NFT markets are among the other advantages of this platform.

# 10. Problems Defi Solves

This chapter addresses DeFi's concrete solutions to the five flaws of traditional finance: inefficiency, limited access, opacity, centralized control, and lack of interoperability.

## INEFFICIENCY

The first of the five flaws of traditional finance is inefficiency. DeFi can handle financial transactions with high volumes of assets and low friction that would generally be a large organizational burden for traditional finance. It does this by creating dApps: reusable smart contracts designed to execute a specific financial operation and available to any user who seeks that type of service, for example, to execute a put option, regardless of the size of the transaction. A user can largely self-serve within the parameters of the smart contract and of the blockchain the application lives on. In the case of Ethereum-based DeFi, the contracts can be used by anyone who pays the flat gas fee, currently around $3 for a transfer and $12 for a dApp feature such as leveraging against collateral. Once deployed, these contracts continually provide their service with near-zero organizational overhead.

### Keepers

Keepers are external participants directly incentivized to provide a service to DeFi protocols, such as monitoring positions to safeguard that they are sufficiently collateralized or triggering state updates for various functions. To ensure that a dApp's benefits and services are optimally priced, keeper rewards are often structured as an auction. Pure, open competition provides value to DeFi platforms by guaranteeing users pay the market price for the services they need.

### Forking

Another concept that also incentivizes efficiency is a **fork**. In the context of open-source code, this occurs when the code is copied and reused with upgrades or enhancements layered on top. A common fork in blockchain protocols is formed when they are referenced in two parallel currencies and chains. Doing so creates competition at the protocol level and creates the best possible smart contract platform. Not only is the code of the entire Ethereum blockchain public and forkable, but each DeFi dApp built on top of Ethereum is as well. Should inefficient or suboptimal DeFi applications exist, the code can be easily copied, improved, and redeployed through forking. Forking and its benefits arise from the open nature of DeFi and blockchains.

Forking creates an interesting challenge to DeFi platforms, namely, **vampirism**: an exact or near-carbon copy of a DeFi platform designed to poach liquidity or users by offering larger incentives than the platform it is copying. Users might be attracted to the higher potential reward for the same functionality, which would cause a reduction in usage and liquidity on the initial platform.

If the inflationary rewards are flawed, with prolonged use the clone could perhaps collapse after a large asset bubble or could select closer-to-optimal models and replace the original platform. Vampirism is not an inherent risk or flaw but rather a complicating factor arising from the pure competition and openness of DeFi. The selection process will eventually give rise to more robust financial infrastructure with optimal efficiency.

## LIMITED ACCESS

As smart contract platforms move to more scalable implementations, user friction falls, enabling a wide range of users and thus mitigating the second flaw of traditional finance: limited access. DeFi gives large, underserved groups like the global unbanked population and small businesses that employ substantial portions of the workforce (e.g., nearly 50 percent in the United States) direct access to financial services. The resulting impact on the entire global economy should be strongly positive. Even consumers who have access to traditional financial services such as bank accounts, mortgages, and credit cards cannot get products with the most competitive pricing and most favorable terms because they are restricted to large institutions. DeFi allows all users access to the entirety of its financial infrastructure, regardless of their wealth or geographic location.

### Yield Farming

Yield farming provides access to many who need financial services but whom traditional finance leaves behind. It provides users with inflationary or contract-funded rewards for staking capital or using a protocol, which are then payable in the same underlying asset the user holds or in a distinct asset such as a governance token. Any user can participate, staking an amount of any size – regardless of how small – and receiving a proportional reward. This capability is particularly powerful in the case of governance tokens. A user of a protocol that issues a governance token via yield farming becomes a partial owner of the platform through the issued token. A rare occurrence in traditional finance, this process is a common and celebrated way to give ownership of the platform to the people who use and benefit from it.

### Initial DeFi Offering

An interesting consequence of yield farming is that a user can create an **initial DeFi offering** (IDO) by market making their own Uniswap trading pair. They can set the initial exchange rate by becoming the first liquidity provider on the pair. Suppose the user's token is called DFT and has a total supply of 2 million. They can make each DFT worth 0.10 USDC by opening the market with 1 million DFT and 100,000 USDC. Any ERC20 token holder can purchase DFT, which drives up the price. As the only liquidity provider, the user also receives all the trading fees. In this way, they can get their token immediate access to as many users as possible. The method sets an artificial price floor for the token if the user controls the supply outside of the amount supplied to the Uniswap market and, as such, inhibits price discovery. The trade-offs of an IDO should be weighed as an option, or strategy, for a user's token distribution.

IDOs democratize access to DeFi in two ways. First, an IDO allows a project to list on high-traffic DeFi exchanges that do not have barriers to entry beyond the initial capital. Second, an IDO allows a user access to the best new projects immediately after the project lists.

## OPACITY

The third drawback of traditional finance is opacity. DeFi elegantly solves this problem through the open and contractual nature of agreements. We will explore how smart contracts and tokenization improve transparency within DeFi.

### Smart Contracts

Smart contracts provide an immediate benefit in terms of transparency. All parties are aware of the capitalization of their counterparties and, to the extent required, can see how funds will be deployed. They can each read the contract, agree on the terms, and eliminate any ambiguity. This transparency substantially eases the threat of legal burdens and brings peace of mind to smaller players who, in the current environment of traditional finance, could be abused by powerful counterparties through delaying or even completely withholding their end of a financial agreement. Realistically, the average consumer does not understand the contract code but can rely on the open-source nature of the platform, the existence of code audits (discussed later) and the wisdom of the crowd to feel secure. Overall, DeFi mitigates counterparty risk and thus creates a host of efficiencies not present under traditional finance.

DeFi participants are accountable for acting in accordance with the terms of the contracts they use. One mechanism for ensuring the appropriate behavior is **staking**, in which a cryptoasset is escrowed into a contract and released to the appropriate counterparty only after the terms are met or is returned to the original holder. Parties can be required to stake on any claims or interactions they make. Staking enforces agreements by imposing a tangible penalty for the misbehaving side and a tangible reward for the counterparty, the latter of which should be as good as or even better than the outcome of the original terms of the contract. These transparent incentive structures provide much more secure and more obvious guarantees than traditional financial agreements.

Another type of smart contract in DeFi that improves transparency is a **token contract**, which allows users to know exactly how many tokens are in the system and the parameters of inflation and deflation.

## CENTRALIZED CONTROL

The fourth flaw of traditional finance is the strong control exerted by governments and large institutions that hold a virtual monopoly over elements such as the money supply, rate of inflation, and access to the best investment opportunities. DeFi upends this centralized control by relinquishing control to open protocols with transparent and immutable properties. The community of stakeholders or even a predetermined algorithm can control a DeFi dApp's parameter, such as the inflation rate. If a dApp contains special privileges for an administrator, all users are aware of the privileges, and any user can readily create a less centralized competitor.

The open-source ethos of blockchain and the public nature of all smart contracts assures that flaws and inefficiencies in a DeFi project can be readily identified and "forked away" by users who copy and improve the flawed project. Consequently, DeFi strives to design protocols that naturally and elegantly incentivize stakeholders and maintain a healthy equilibrium through careful mechanism design. Naturally, there are trade-offs in having and not having a centralized party. Centralized control allows for radically decisive action in a crisis, which may or may not be the appropriate reaction. The path to decentralizing finance will certainly involve growing pains because of the challenges in pre-planning for every eventuality and economic nuance. Ultimately, however, the transparency and security a decentralized approach brings will lead to robust protocols that can become trusted financial infrastructure for a global user base.

### Decentralized Autonomous Organization

In a **decentralized autonomous organization** (DAO), the rules of operation are encoded in smart contracts that determine who can execute what behavior or upgrade. It is common for a DAO to have some kind of **governance token**, which gives an owner some percentage of the vote on future outcomes. We will explore governance in much more detail later.

## LACK OF INTEROPERABILITY

We will now touch on how DeFi solves for the lack of interoperability that exists in traditional finance. Traditional financial products are difficult to integrate, generally requiring at minimum a wire transfer and many cases unable to be recombined. The possibilities for DeFi are substantial, and new innovations continue to grow exponentially, fueled by how easy it is to compose DeFi products. Once a base infrastructure has been established – for example, to create a synthetic asset – any new protocols allowing for borrowing and lending can be applied. A higher layer would allow for attainment of leverage on top of borrowed assets. Such composability can continue in an increasing number of directions as new platforms arise. For this reason, **DeFi Legos** is an analogy often used to describe the act of combining existing protocols into a new protocol. The next section discusses tokenization and networked liquidity, which are advantages to this composability.

### Tokenization

Tokenization is a critical way DeFi platforms integrate. Take, for example, a percentage ownership stake in a private commercial real estate venture. It would be quite difficult in traditional finance to use this asset as collateral for a loan or as margin to open a levered derivative position. Because DeFi relies on shared interfaces, applications can directly plug into each other's assets, repackage, and subdivide positions as needed. DeFi has the potential to unlock liquidity in traditionally illiquid assets through tokenization. A simple use case would be creating fractional shares from a unitary asset such as a stock. We can extend this concept to give fractional ownership to scarce resources such as rare art. The tokens can be used as collateral for any other DeFi service, such as leverage or derivatives.

We can invert this paradigm to create token bundles of groups of real-world or digital assets and trade them like an ETF. Imagine a dApp like a real estate investment trust (REIT), but with the added capability of allowing the owner to subdivide the REIT into the individual real estate components to select a preferred geographic distribution and allocation within the REIT. Owning the token means overseeing how the properties are distributed. The token can be traded on a decentralized exchange to liquidate the position.

Compared with digital assets, tokenizing hard assets, such as real estate or precious metals, is more difficult because the practical considerations such as maintenance and storage cannot be enforced by code. Legal restrictions across jurisdictions are also a challenge for tokenization; nevertheless, the utility of secure, contractual tokenization for most use cases should not be underestimated.

A tokenized version of a position in a DeFi platform is a pluggable derivative asset that is usable in another platform. Tokenization allows the benefits and features of one position to be portable. The archetypal example of portability through tokenization is Compound, which allows for robust lending markets in which a position – itself a token – can accrue variable-rate interest denominated in a given token. If, for example, the base asset is ETH, the ETH deposit wrapper known as cETH (cToken) can be used in place of the base asset. The result is an ETH-backed derivative that is also accruing variable-rate interest per the Compound protocol. Tokenization therefore unlocks new revenue models for dApps because they can plug asset holdings directly into Compound or use the cToken interface to gain the benefits of Compound's interest rates.

## Networked Liquidity

The concept of interoperability extends easily to liquidity in the exchange use case. Traditional exchanges – in particular those that retail investors typically use – cannot readily share liquidity with other exchanges. In DeFi, as a subcomponent of the contract, any exchange application can leverage the liquidity and rates of any other exchange on the same blockchain. This capability allows for networked liquidity and leads to very competitive rates for users within the same application.

# 11. The Future Of Decentralized Finance (Defi)

Before we proceed, let's take a brief look at some of the things Defi enables us to do:

- Transparency: A financial environment that is transparent and auditable.
- Accessibility: Unrestricted access to Defi apps without fear of discrimination based on race, gender, beliefs, nationality, or geographic location.
- Efficient: Programmable money allows for the elimination of centralized middlemen, resulting in a more economical and efficient financial market.
- Convenience: For a modest price and with little waiting time, money may now be transmitted anywhere, at any time, and to anybody who has access to a cryptocurrency wallet.

All of those mentioned above have enabled users to accomplish the following: supply liquidity to earn yields on unproductive assets with no maturation/lock-in period, obtain loans (with collateral) without paperwork and repay them whenever they want, and quickly execute automated trading methods. The best part is that all of the above may be accessible by anybody, anywhere, anytime, as long as they have Internet connectivity. That is the power of Defi in terms of accessibility, and we are only at the beginning of this adventure.

According to the blockchain platform Dune Analytics statistics, the number of Defi users climbed from 93,000 in January 2020 to 1.8 million in April 2021. The market's valuation climbed from $700 million to $58 billion during the same period. Despite emerging to the surface during a stock market meltdown and a pandemic, decentralized finance became the industry's next big thing. Defi transcended its niche status and completely dispelled the worry of becoming another ICO-like phenomenon. Furthermore, its vicious performance was frightening enough to frighten crypto's centralized exchanges, which have lost a major portion of liquidity to DEXs.

DeFi's disruptive potential is undeniable. A new decentralized future is upon us, which should come as no surprise in the blockchain sector. However, there are other challenges that must be addressed before we can achieve widespread adoption.

Smart contracts continue to be vulnerable to exploits, anonymous developers continue to act like vultures by starting rug pull initiatives, and the threat of laws continues to loom over our heads. For the time being, Defi is the wild west of crypto, and both creators and users must reach a specific degree of maturity for the specialized ecosystem to establish itself as a prominent and serious sector in this new decade.

It will take several years to achieve a perfected and balanced state, and the timing will be fully dependent on the community and its conduct. In these unpredictable and chaotic times, it seems apparent that disruptive technologies are more likely than ever to enter the actual world and that this is our opportunity to make significant changes. The road may be long and difficult, but one thing is certain: the future of finance is decentralized.

Individual users will not wish to conduct their transactions across several platforms. Users will mostly congregate around on-ramps (for example, exchanges) and wallets (e.g., balance.io). Because these initiatives are open-source and decentralized, they will be able to interface with one another to enable trade, storage of existing assets, insurance, and other functions within the same platform. We're seeing some early variants of this, such as Trust Wallet interacting with Dapps. Platforms such as Morpher.io and Abra are beginning to integrate traditional instruments such as equities with tokens, which will play a significant role in allowing people in remote parts of the world to gain access to previously unattainable foreign assets. De-Fi platforms may, over time, reduce the complexity created by regulators in the goal of keeping economies walled off, allowing regular investors without the appropriate instruments (e.g., specialist banks) to gain access to commodities, exotic assets, derivatives, foreign currencies, and even equity.

The Defi ecosystem as a whole is estimated to be worth roughly $1 billion. Today, the majority of this is provided through MakerDAO. If we use token market capitalization as a proxy, it is worth less than 1% of the overall ecosystem, based on the total market capitalization of $173 billion. However, decentralized banking is one of the few areas where a tokenized product is used regularly. It can restore utility tokens' "utility." Decentralized finance has the potential to enable applications that were thought to be achievable in 2013 but difficult to develop due to scaling issues and volatility. The advent of reliable tokens, payment systems, and lending platforms might create opportunities for businesses worldwide and bring our financial markets closer together while enhancing transparency. While there is significant systemic danger in these systems (e.g., Dai locked up with eth, used to buy Eth), they provide an alternative to the banks, which may have put an entire generation in jeopardy with their CDOs in 2008. It is far too early to declare any of them the clear victors. However, it may be premature to conclude that Defi will not add value to the ecosystem.

When entrepreneurs traveled far and wide in pursuit of new opportunities 400 years ago, they issued stock as a method for individuals to share the risks and rewards of new companies. It democratized access to wealth-creation tools. When Satoshi Nakamoto released the Bitcoin code ten years ago, he developed a financial system that ensured an individual's money stayed theirs.

Decentralized finance is the natural progression of the same. It has the potential to bring our markets closer together than ever before, to eliminate needless middlemen, to provide significant cost efficiencies, and to open access to populations that have previously been underserved.

It, like the web, will first serve a privileged few, but its benefits will be passed on to an entire generation of underserved consumers who may never have had access to loans or the ability to make international payments. If macro trends such as the gig economy and globalization continue, the necessary financial infrastructure must be put in place.

We have our first true shot at making it happen with decentralized money. When Satoshi published Bitcoin's whitepaper, banks were on the verge of yet another bailout. Decentralized finance expands on his idea of providing individuals with dignity, sovereignty, and transparency over the storage and investment of their hard-earned money. It isn't the establishment's anti-banking stance. It is the consumer-friendly option.

And by constructing it, one is not undermining the power of the government or banks but rather enabling the common man to have an option in an ecosystem where none has existed for millennia.

## The Defi User Experience

While access to Defi apps may be a non-issue, the whole user experience remains one of DeFi's key pain points. Having said that, numerous teams throughout the world are working hard to improve the experience. Examine some of them and the problems they are seeking to solve:

Wallet: Argent is developing a dramatically improved user-focused crypto wallet experience, including free Ethereum transactions without the requirement for ETH, native integration with Compound (and others), and the elimination of seed keys.

Product participation: DeFiZap abstracts away many of the intricacies and stages required with Defi products, allowing customers to access various financial products in a single transaction, saving time and effort.

Gelato Finance has announced their “If this, then that” cryptocurrency development. It essentially allows users to define actions that will be carried out when specific criteria are satisfied, such as "Buy ETH when it is $200" or "Send some money to Alice on her birthday."

Insurance: The financial market successfully facilitates risk transfer. Another person's profit is another person's hedge against his position. As previously discussed, insurance is now available through Nexus Mutual or Opyn. If you're prepared to accept a lower yield on money you've put into lending mechanisms like Compound in exchange for peace of mind, it's now possible.

Liquidity aggregation: There are numerous decentralized exchanges (DEXes) in the market, each with differing liquidity, making it difficult for customers to determine which one is ideal for their trade. With liquidity aggregators like 1inch.exchange, Paraswap, and DEX.AG that help to automatically divide orders between DEXes to assure the best possible prices, this is progressively becoming a thing of the past.

Yield optimization: Do you remember shopping around for the greatest rates on fixed deposits at various banks? In Defi, yield bouncers like idle.finance, DeFiSaver, and iEarn automatically distribute your crypto assets to the Ethereum blockchain locations with the best yield possibilities.

While there is currently no single "killer app" that bridges the user experience divide, we believe it is not far away!

# Conclusion

Decentralized Finance is focused on building financial services separate from the traditional financial and political system. This would take into consideration a more open financial framework and might actually forestall precedents of censorship and discrimination from one side of the world to the other.

While an enticing thought, not all things benefit from decentralization.

Finding the use cases that are generally appropriate for the attributes of blockchains is vital in building a valuable heap of open financial products.

I want to get this information out to as many people as possible because I believe DeFi is a force that will be disrupting finance in the near future. If you enjoyed the book and found it helpful, please leave me a review. Thanks!

www.ingramcontent.com/pod-product-compliance
Lightning Source LLC
LaVergne TN
LVHW082359200926
848481LV00012B/3616
* 9 7 9 8 2 0 1 1 0 6 4 0 9 *